MW01297211

Know Your Worth, Get Your Worth

Know Your Worth, Get Your Worth

SALARY NEGOTIATION FOR WOMEN

OLIVIA JARAS

•

Know Your Worth, Get Your Worth Copyright © 2017 by Olivia Jaras.

Dedicated To

To my mom, I can only hope that I will raise my daughters to be as strong and resilient as you.
To all the women out there who have failed but are still willing to take a chance on themselves—may the world be your oyster.

Contents

Preface

If you bought this book, you're probably in a situation where either you or a woman you know isn't being fairly compensated. You've probably overheard that your peers earn more than you do, or you might have even tried to ask for a raise only to have it blow up in your face, and not get anything but resentment out of having asked.

Guess what? Millions of us have been there. So take a deep breath and read on.

Are there a whole lot of books out there that will help you learn to negotiate? Yes. But do they help you figure out what you are *worth*? No. **Well, what's the point in negotiating if you don't know what you are asking for?**

Beyond empowerment and support, this book gives you the insider secrets to quantifying your value in today's market and tools to discover (and *get*) your worth. Welcome to your front row seat to the world of compensation and salary-setting.

I spent the better part of a decade setting salaries and working behind the scenes in the world of compensation for both men and women. I rarely observed a woman speak up on her own behalf for a promotion or a raise. If she did speak up, insecurities and uncertainties would usually get the better of her, dropping her right back at her starting point at the first sign of pushback. If somehow she managed to push her way through, she would leave her counterpart with a bitter impression that tarnished future negotiations. This is how millions of women find themselves to be just another statistic. They've either been burned before, avoid asking for fear of rejection, or ask so aggressively that they tarnish their chances of future negotiations.

This book treats the symptoms, discusses the cause, and ultimately gives you the much-needed medicine so that you can not only advocate for yourself, but also help pay it forward and encourage other women to know their worth and know how to ask for it.

My mission in this book is to empower you to take action by teaching you the secrets of compensation and the art of gender-based negotiation. Master these secrets, and you will know your worth and get your worth. So read on my friend, there's no time like now to be informed, feel empowered, and get a raise.

"It's indisputable that there's a real pay gap. People can argue about how big, but that's almost besides the point. The point is that every woman, every girl, deserves to get paid what they're worth." —Sheryl Sandberg

Introduction

> I do not demand equal pay for any women save those who do equal work in value. Scorn to be coddled by your employers; make them understand that you are in their service as workers, not as women. —Susan B. Anthony

The gender card is not a good enough excuse to not know what you're worth.

The gender inequality issue has been a prevalent and blatant part of our society since the beginning of time immemorial. Many have traced gender inequality in the workplace to the industrial revolution, but the truth is we have been selling ourselves short for much longer.

Just a cursory look at early Roman history will show you that, by the time our calendar began in the year Dot, women were already expected to be homemakers, staying chaste; and they could not participate in politics or engage in the same types of jobs as men. If we rewind a little further to hunter-gatherer times, you will also see that women were expected to stay home rearing children, doing less threatening work while men were out doing the hunting.

There's nothing wrong with being culturally assigned a role—after all, these assignments have led to the marvellous world we live in today. My point with this narrative is to show that, at a global scale, gender inequality has been part of our cultural making since the beginning of history. Sad, but true!

Fast-forward a few thousand years and everything has changed... Well, almost everything. We've entered an era where governments and companies are increasingly trying to make male and female equality the new norm. There are laws that protect women from discrimination in the workforce and in society. Many employers offer flexible work schedules and extended leave to accommodate working moms. Yet there's still a gap. Why?

In our time, anyone haughty enough to hold on to the thought that women are limited beings who are not quite capable of measuring up to men is sure to face an onslaught of criticism and social marginalization that they would not have expected fifty years ago (think *Madmen* series).

I haven't yet met a woman who isn't a fierce advocate for her family and her children, a present and steadfast ruthless negotiator for those closest to her. But, place her out in the world of advocating and negotiating for herself, and she will usually fall short, stand down, or walk away from the opportunity!

She suddenly goes from a passionate and fierce advocate to an unassertive fly on the wall who doesn't feel comfortable asking for what she really wants and deserves. Nowhere is this more obvious than when negotiating for salaries.

Hundreds of books have been written on the topic of gender-based negotiations and gender inequality, but we still haven't made a dent in the gender wage gap (Ladies, we've been in the 70% range since the '70s... That was almost 50 years ago). WHY?

Most of these resources are well-intentioned and meant to empower women, but they are simply misinformed with regards to how to understand your worth. As a woman, you can read all the empowering literature out there, but if you don't feel confident about the number you are asking for, you will be instantly deflated when you receive pushback from your negotiation counterpart. Knowing your worth beyond any doubt allows you to strategically push your way through a tough negotiation. Until now, none of the folks writing these books have taken the compensation component of your negotiation seriously. Until now, most of the books out there about leaning in and negotiating have good intent, but they don't address what you're actually worth! What's the point of leaning in to negotiate if you don't know what you are asking for?

Knowing your value in the market is not as simple as Googling it or asking someone in a similar job what they think you should earn—but you wouldn't know this unless you are an insider within the compensation industry.

This knowledge is something that only the folks hiring and setting your salaries tend to know. Most companies have an entire compensation team doing due diligence, researching surveys, and working with market pricing tools to come up with what you should earn relative to the position description, their budget, internal equity, and the market.

As a mother of two daughters, wife of an army veteran, and a proud Chilean-American, I can relate to how women will fight hard for friendships and family, but seemingly disconnect as soon as they place a foot on the career ladder. This a problem all women have: We are great at negotiating for others, but not for ourselves. Deeply ingrained societal expectations and culture drive us to be communal and caring—and we forget about ourselves. It's hard to change something we aren't even aware of, so let's work on it together!

This problem is even further aggravated for those of us in minority groups. As a Latina, I've had a front row seat observing how women, and particularly female minorities, get relegated to the caboose of the salary train. This is not because the employer doesn't want to pay equally, but because we just don't know or we have a hard time believing in what we are worth, so we don't ask for it in the first place.

Companies don't simply Google what you should earn and call it a day. They do their research and so should you. In this book, I will demystify the compensation process for you, give you the tools to value yourself accurately in today's market, and help you develop your own strategy as to how to advocate or negotiate for what you are truly worth.

In 2015, the US Census Bureau reported that, relative to every dollar earned by white, non-Hispanic men, full-time, year-round workers, Latinas make only 55 cents, Asian American women 84 cents, and white, non-Hispanic women 75 cents.

After being an insider for many years, it became evident that women at all career levels need a little help at the negotiating table.

If you don't need salary coaching for yourself, then I applaud you, but we need your help helping other women. Help us bring other women above the gap and start negotiating for their worth. Share, inspire, and pay it forward. We need your help to close the gap one woman at a time.

This is your chance to be part of a broader movement and let your voice be heard. Take time to educate yourself, share your story, support your female friends, colleagues, and family, encourage them to learn about their worth and get paid what they deserve. For more tools to help women negotiate, go to salarycoaching.com.

I encourage you to read on, learn, listen, relate, and finally take a stand for yourself and start negotiating for your worth.

Chapter 1

KNOW YOUR WORTH

"Why would anyone pay you what you are not asking for? Successfully negotiating your salary means knowing your worth and knowing how to ask for it." —Olivia Jaras

Conquering Our Fears and Choosing to Negotiate

The day I realized that closing the gender wage gap was my calling, I was sitting in the office of one of the most powerful women in business—well within the C-suite of her company (in other words: a top executive). She was at the helm of a 4 billion (yes billion) dollar operation.

We were working on a fairly routine reorganization of one of her departments, and I had already thanked her for her time. After I told her that I'd look into the salary data for her staff and make sure that everyone was squared away, she said, "I need to ask your help with a more personal question...." I froze.

We barely knew each other, so I wasn't quite sure where this was going. She went on to say, "I met with my equivalents from other organizations last week at a summit, and it became apparent that I am terribly underpaid relative to all those men."

I had access to the data right there on my laptop, so I looked at the salary information relevant to her market and, indeed, she was being paid absurdly low relative to what her male counterparts were earning.

I actually felt pity for an incredibly powerful woman and asked her what I end up asking most women I meet with, "Did you negotiate your salary when you took the job several years ago?"

"Not really," she responded. "I just took what they offered me, thinking it would be fair. Truthfully, I was just excited to get the role."

My heart sank for her.

On one end, I could hardly feel that her current salary of several hundreds of thousands of dollars could be perceived as "unfair." Yet she was known for being one of the best in the industry, and here she was earning only 20% of what some of her peers were earning.

It turns out she took what had been offered to her at the time, assuming she could not negotiate. She knew she was worth a lot of money, but didn't really know how to narrow down an exact number.

So, as is the case with many women, she assumed anywhere within the six-figures range would work fine. For someone who had made it so far up the career ladder, I was shocked that she had been in the dark about her worth for so long.

Research, research, research, and the truth

Over the next few months, I began deliberately looking back at the female recommendations I had made across companies I had worked for. I noticed that, in most cases, if I had recommended a hiring range (in other words, there was wiggle room in the salary to allow for negotiating), most women would invariably be below the 50th percentile of my recommendation, while men would be at or above the 50th percentile.

I took it upon myself to talk with hiring managers and compensation analysts in a vast spread of industries where salaries could have been negotiated. I asked them to look at their numbers and see if they noticed a pattern. If so, what did they think caused it?

Sadly, my prediction came true. There, in real dollars, women were being hired in at a drastically lower salary percentile than men, and the most common reaction from hiring managers I came across was, "She didn't negotiate the offer, she actually seemed thrilled to get the job."

It was a disheartening realization, because I knew that on my end, probably like every other compensation analyst out there, I had done a very thorough job ensuring that my recommendations were fair, and that they were gender- and race-neutral.

I also knew the institutions for whom I was setting salaries had no intention of perpetuating the gender wage gap, nor was anyone involved trying to bypass government equal pay standards. So how did this happen?

Sadly, when it came to negotiating salaries, women were simply not showing up.

Fast forward to the present day and to the time of writing this book.

Here to help

I've helped hundreds of underpaid women re-negotiate and earn what they are worth in the market. From figuring out that they were in the wrong job to begin with, to getting over $250,000 more than what they were originally earning, I've been a part of all types of negotiating scenarios.

Invariably, I find that my clients allow their insecurities to seep through in the face of a negotiation, and their salaries suffer. Women are being underpaid in many instances because they are allowing the socially-ingrained notion that they are not good enough creep into their decision-making skills.

Don't get me wrong, I don't condone pretending you don't have weaknesses, nor do I suggest you ignore working on them. **But the reality is that, if you assess yourself as a measure of your weaknesses rather than your strengths, that's how others will measure you as well.**

Our insecurities tend to bleed through our words and our actions, and if you don't think you are worth it, why should anyone else?

You need to accept your flaws and own your strengths. Believing in yourself is part of it, but unfortunately for women, we also have to be very deliberate about how we communicate that we are owning our strengths.

Maybe things will change one day, but until then, it is socially ill-received when women are overtly confident. As we know from experience, it is all too often received as egocentric and entitled. We will delve more into this challenge in further chapters.

So when it comes to salary negotiations, our insecurities are furthered by not having the right information to help us figure out what we are worth. At some point in your career (if it hasn't happened yet), someone will have the best intentions in advising you to go find out what you are worth on a free online salary survey source. But this advice is wrong and, in most cases, detrimental. Many companies have an entire compensation department, if not a compensation person within their human resources area, that solely focuses on figuring out what it is that the company should pay its employees.

Free online salary survey sources have noble intentions, yet they are rarely as accurate or specific as you would hope or need their data to be. Data is generically gathered and formed into a figure that will not actually be relevant or specific enough for you and your circumstance. While these websites have their place in showing a very broad picture, do not rely on them for accurate data on your market value.

Truth be told, compensation experts will usually dismiss the accuracy of these free data sources. Most companies spend thousands of dollars on paid market data in order to set salaries; and their compensation experts spend quite some time setting your salary by analyzing your résumé relative to the position description, the market, and internal equity (more on this later).

Bottom line, these compensation folks don't simply Google what it is that you should earn and call it a day. Neither should you. It's like showing up to compete at a monster truck race with your plastic toy truck.

But fear not! This book is my way of sitting down for a cup of coffee with you and walking you through the entire negotiation process. I will take you behind the scenes of the compensation world and help you understand what really goes on in the black hole that is HR. Then, I will show you how to figure out what you are worth and how to ask for it.

What do we mean by market worth?

When talking about your market worth/market value, we are essentially referring to the price tag on your skill set and abilities, relative to a specific position, at a specific point in time, in a specific market and industry, as compared to talent that is already out there performing a similar job.

Let's get started.

First, let's get in the right mindset for you to maximize what you get out of this book.

The following are not hard fast rules, but rather basic reflections on what most women face every day notoriously in our careers. They will come in handy as I help you figure out your market value and negotiation strategy. When that little nagging voice of insecurity in your head creeps back up (as it inevitably will), feel free to come back to these pages.

Stop making excuses for selling yourself short.

Thinking about what they are worth in the market usually makes my clients' stomachs lurch just a little... and then they turn to excuses:

"Oh, I earn less because I need to leave earlier to pick up my kids."

"I have four kids, and usually one of them is sick, so then I usually have to work from home."

"I'm not that good at what I do."

Self-doubt is prevalent in the everyday life of women. Accept this and move on with determination to no longer be left behind. If you need to negotiate peripheral things such as a flexible schedule, bring that to the table. But your salary, as measured by the time you dedicate to work, should be a separately-negotiated item.

It takes guts to accept that it's time you should be measured with the same yardstick as others. Yes, the same yardstick as other men *and* women. Knowing your value and accepting what you are worth in your career can be hard to realize, but knowing this gives us a baseline when we show up at a negotiation.

Peripheral and non-compensable items can be brought to the table as well, but that shouldn't mean that you are less valuable.

In fact, most of my clients who need flexible schedules because of their family end up voluntarily putting in way more hours of work at home than if they worked an "inflexible" schedule.

Knowing their value has given all my clients a backbone reinforcement when they receive pushback in a negotiation. We've all heard knowledge is power, but it's of no real use if you don't apply this knowledge and take action. In our case, knowing your market value is empowering, knowing how to ask for it is what makes you powerful.

The fact is that, even if you are unemployed, you will have a market value relative to a position that is heavily dependent upon many factors, which we will come to later in this book.

Decide to get off the hamster wheel and take action

Why make a fuss... our career is moving along nicely and you really enjoy your job... Sure, you haven't received a pay raise in five years other than an annual increase which barely keeps up with cost of living, but you'll be recognized at some point.... Right?

Think again. If you don't look out for yourself, no one else will do it for you. But hold your horses! You have to be sly and strategic in order to break free. This book is your secret weapon, so don't tell them about it... just read on!

Know your strengths and weaknesses

We are all really good at a handful of things and completely useless at many more. I'm really good at connecting with people one-on-one, understanding their issues and helping to solve them, some would say it's my "thing."

Too often women yield in a negotiation because they don't fulfill all of their job accountabilities perfectly. "Oh, I really don't know how to do pivot tables in Excel very well...." and she therefore thinks this should be a sticking issue that drives what she earns.

If doing pivot tables is the main accountability of the position, then she's probably in the wrong job. But if the role requires primarily (and she is good at) customer service, memo writing, and needle threading, these are the line items that she needs to highlight in her negotiation.

Inadvertently, too many women make their weaknesses the centerpiece of a negotiation. In the workplace, you will ultimately be judged by a measure of your strengths and your weaknesses combined. Perception of how strong your strengths are, along with how weak your weaknesses are, can seal your fate in a negotiation. Your worth to your boss will be measured beyond dollars and cents, you will be judged by a measure of how your strengths and weaknesses are perceived relative to your job role.

How do you stack up to your peers?

How detrimental are your weaknesses and how relevant are your strengths?

Is it just about the money? In the world of compensation, yes it's about what you are worth in terms of dollars and cents. In the world of negotiations, absolutely not. More often than not, you are not only negotiating salary—you are negotiating many other non-compensable factors. Maybe you just want to reduce your hours or ask for flexible work time, squeeze in workouts during lunch, extra vacation days, or unpaid leave?

Knowing your market value and having a strategy can help negotiate all of these factors.

If you are unhappy in your position, the increase in responsibilities, or the hours, no amount of $$$ will get you what you are looking for. That's not to say these things cannot be negotiated; but in these circumstances, money will not buy you out of your problems.

Brace yourself to be resilient

We all hate to hear the word failure, so let's just say it: FAILURE. Now think of the word RESILIENCE. Failure and resilience work in perfect harmony; you can't have one without the other.

By now, life has probably taught you a thing or two about being resilient. We've all failed utterly at some point (if you haven't, please put down this book... denial is a whole separate issue), but we've picked ourselves up and kept trying.

I'll ask you to stop here and think about your three biggest failures to date, and how they've made you a stronger, more resilient woman. Look at those failures in the eye and thank them for a job well done, you wouldn't be who you are today if it weren't for them.

But how does resilience tie into salary negotiations? Well, think about it. Because you've done your research and know what you are worth, it doesn't mean that your employer is going to jump with excitement and pay you that magical number. I almost guarantee you'll receive pushback. In fact, I have seen very few cases where the employer's first reaction was bright and cheery about giving a raise. Brace yourself because the first time around, your strategy to get a raise might not work. But, from that initial pushback, you will gain insight and additional perspective that you can use to return with an even better strategy.

Expect pushback and know that, if your strategy fails the first time around, you'll regroup and reassess for round two.

I have yet to see anyone who has had to go for a third round in order to be paid what they are worth, but if this happens to be your case, be resilient and I promise you'll get there.

Ask yourself these questions and be honest. Write them down and look back at them as you progress through the book.

- How has not knowing your value stopped you from progressing in your career?

- If you knew your market value and had no issues negotiating for it, what impact would this have on your career?

Statistics

If we take the time to really acknowledge the realities of the gender pay gap, it actually makes for scary and, plainly, sad read. More chapters will highlight a scary and real statistic!

Wyoming is the *worst* state when it comes to recognizing and paying women the same as a man. Women earn 36% less than a man for having the same qualifications, doing the same job, and working the same hours.

Wyoming is closely followed by the six worst states for the wage gender gap:

- Louisiana (32%)
- West Virginia (29%)
- Utah (29%)
- North Dakota (29%)
- Montana (27%)
- Oklahoma (27%)

You will need to move to Washington DC or New York to get

closer to being paid the same as your male colleagues, where it is still 13% and 11% less, respectively.

There is yet to be a state where there is no gender pay gap.

Source: US Census Bureau, American Community Survey and the National Women's Law Center.

Chapter 2

WHO SETS THE BOUNTY ON YOUR HEAD?

Human resources are like natural resources; they're often buried deep. You have to go looking for them, they're not just lying around on the surface. —Ken Robinson

Isn't it sad that Human Resources tends to have a reputation of being a big black hole filled with obscure bureaucracies? While that's rarely the intention of any given HR department, that's what HR ends up being perceived as from the outside.

Sadly, the lack of transparency and accountability in many organizations results in HR departments being inefficient and bloated.

For our purposes, you don't need to be clued in on all of the inefficiencies of HR. What you DO need to know is that, behind the scenes of most medium-to-large sized companies, the Hiring Manager or hiring team has sent your résumé to the big black hole that is "HR" so that they can come up with a salary range that can be extended to you.

Essentially, this will mean that your résumé is being looked at through four different lenses:

1. How does your experience stack up to the position description?

2. How do you stack up relative to the market?

3. Could they find someone with your background/abilities locally, or would they need to recruit someone to fill the role?

4. How do you stack up relative to others in the department? (This is called Internal Equity.)

As a compensation expert, I have recommended thousands of salaries, and the majority of these recommendations could have been higher if the résumé was better reflective of the candidate's ability to do the job in question (not cluttered with all your favorite but irrelevant things), that is, focusing on the compensable factors.

Obviously no two companies and HR department will have the same methodology for setting your salary, but the standard process will go roughly along these lines:

Let's assume the company has a HR department. While HR may not be involved in writing the position description, they will likely approve it before it gets posted for the world to see. HR will ensure the position description follows company standards, that funding is available to pay for the added role, that the position is FLSA Compliant, and that the description makes sense relative to the title and needs of the job.

Most companies go through excruciatingly detailed evaluation of every line item within a position description for two good reasons:

- They want to make sure they will attract the right type of candidate. (Although it's worth noting here that, while they have an ideal candidate in their head, when interviews start, they realize many different people could fulfill the role).

- Once you are hired into the position, the description is what you technically will be held against when evaluated for raises and promotions.

Loss of earnings – A cautionary tale

Gina was a Benefits Coordinator at a medium-sized company. She started out in an entry level role, earning $37,000 per year. Within five months, she progressed to managing two interns and then an additional part-time position. Three years went by before she worked up the courage to ask for a raise that was reflective of her change in responsibilities.

The manager agreed that this indeed should be addressed and promptly gave her a 20% raise. Gina and her manager made the appropriate changes to the position description; and Gina brought up the fact that she had been fulfilling these "new" duties for well over two years. Her manager responded that the company policy only allows him to retroactively pay her for the last six months of these "new duties."

Gina missed out on at least two years of an increased salary and any compounded growth that could be tagged on from annual cost of living increases (about 3% of her base salary every year). While unfair, the company is within their rights to enforce the NO in this instance.

So, back to HR posting an open job:

- Once all the standard internal checks are done, the position will be approved for posting.

- Once posted, it will usually be left "live" on job search sites until a sizeable applicant pool is developed (unless a really desirable candidate comes along or they already have someone in mind).

It might take months to develop a strong applicant pool; but if the position is likely to receive many applicants, the pool will fill quickly.

If you come across a posting that is only live for a brief period of time (seven days or so), it is likely the company already had someone in mind for the role, but it was posted in order to be compliant with the law. For this type of posting, candidate profiles are rarely reviewed. However, if your résumé is stellar, you may still have a chance at being called in. More on résumé writing later in the book.

Now let's assume the company does not have a HR department. If you are applying for a job with either a startup company or a small family business, odds are the "HR" department is very informal or non-existent.

While some argue not having a HR function allows a company to do whatever they want and not follow the market, you can turn this around to your advantage by filling the HR gap for the person hiring you.

Think about it! The person hiring you likely has another role at the company other than hiring—they are having to fulfill their job as well as the HR function.

They could use some breathing room from their overloaded plate. If from the onset of the interview, the person interviewing you perceives you as a solution to their problems, you're on the right track to get what you want.

Knowledge + Power + Action = Success

Knowledge is not power, the implementation of knowledge is power! Knowing your company setup is key to beating the game.

How being informed can get you the job

Becky had re-entered the workforce after three years of staying home with her children. She had studied accounting in college and became the bookkeeper for a medium-sized company in two different locations, which later expanded to three. This made accounting tricky.

An opportunity came from a restaurant owner in Miami that was expanding and opening two more locations and needed someone urgently to do the bookkeeping. Until now, the owner's wife had been managing the books with no real bookkeeping background, but she was ready to pass this job on to someone who would be more qualified.

During her phone interview, Becky realized that, while the expansion was an exciting time for the restaurant owner, the accounting and bookkeeping of such an operation was stressing him out. He had never hired someone to do the books and did not know how to pay someone to do the job.

Becky took this opportunity to prepare for the in-person interview by reaching out to other restaurant owners in the area, asking how they had expanded and how their bookkeeping was impacted.

She contacted bookkeepers and accountants in the food industry, asked what they were earning, what schedule they were working, and what size operation they were running. In other words, she did her research. Becky was informed.

When she showed up to the in-person interview, Becky was able to guide the distressed owner into the salary she wanted and the flexible hours she needed by addressing his worries, while reassuring the bookkeeping would be in great hands. Needless to say, she got the job.

Form your strategy based on knowledge

When dealing with a small company, don't assume anything, but KNOW everything you can in order to fill in the information gaps for your interviewer when the right opportunity presents itself. In later chapters you will learn how to use the interviewer's body language to determine if you are building rapport with them or not.

Carry out your own investigative research to understand the HR structure or even the circumstance of the position. It really will feel like seeing the forest through the trees.

Researching a company you are working for already OR a new company you are heading to for an interview will make you stand out from other average applicants. Don't feel too overwhelmed if you don't really know what you are doing in terms of research; just have fun investigating and playing detective.

"If we knew what it was we were doing, it would not be called research" —Albert Einstein

If you take the time to carry out basic research, the knowledge will give you a competitive edge and will ultimately make you feel ready and able to generate leverage from the information you have found.

Meet Megan—Research pays off!

Megan applied for a customer service position that required her to answer phones and emails in a very courteous and polite way. Megan did her research and found out that the company had recently undergone some hard times with the food product that they sold. They were forced to recall a large number of their products because they were contaminated with some unhealthy bacteria. Obviously, it had not been the intention of the company to sell product that wasn't up to standards, but in the food industry, these things happen. This inevitably led to a flurry of customer service calls and emails (hence the reason they were hiring for this role).

Being armed with this knowledge, Megan was able to prepare herself for the interview, addressing the people in a way that she could convey her preparedness in the case of a similar crisis.

Essentially, she was able to use the information about the recall to formulate her own strategy: that they could rely on her to be a functional and effective way to mitigate any kind of hardships, not to mention everyday customer service.

Megan got an offer on the spot!

Let's start the journey to forming your strategy: Coaching Tips!

- Make a list of what you know and what don't you know about the company. Who's the current CEO or owner?
  - This information is vital to understanding the vision and mission to which the company currently ascribes. At the very top, folks are setting the strategy for where this company is headed, and you need to understand this strategy in order to know how you can contribute.

- What is the HR setup? Do they have a compensation structure or compensation philosophy? A salary structure? Check their website. If so, write it down.

- What size are they? Can you figure out what their revenue is, or their employee headcount?

- Look at the company website's "About us" section or read their blog. Google them. Have they been in the news lately? What for?

- Review all the places the company shares information (social media) and get a feel for their tone and the way they communicate. This gives you insight into the type of culture they are striving for.

- Review the LinkedIn profiles of the people who are interviewing you and get a feel for common interests.
    - Your gut reaction might be to avoid clicking on their profiles so they don't know that you're looking, but think of it this way: they should be glad that you looked at their profiles and informed yourself before the interview. You actually cared enough to do your due diligence.
    - If you currently work at the company, involve your colleagues. If you feel comfortable, why not ask a colleague or friend, "How am I acting in the work environment? Am I in line with the direction of our company? Do I embody the vision and mission?" Sometimes an outside perspective can offer more clarity. Ultimately, even if their answers don't mean anything for your strategy, at least you are setting the tone

of caring and being consciously in line with the company. Remember, word travels fast, especially around the water cooler.

- What do you know about your manager, or the person you would be reporting to? Are there any reviews or information out there that could give you a sense of his or her personality?
  - If you have had zero practice in reading people, we will get to this in a later chapter.

- Finally, practice your answers out loud.

While you do your research, many questions may arise about the company and about yourself, some to answer now and some to ask in the interview (rehearse, rehearse, rehearse!). As more questions arise, write them down and answer them. They will be a useful tool as you work through this book and start to form your strategy.

So what do I do now?

After all this research, you'll probably be wondering, "So, what do I do with all this information?" Your research will allow you the solid, rational footing to say, "I want to work at your company," or, "I want that raise because...." If you don't have factual information backing you up when you go to negotiate, any case you try to make will come across as weak and driven by emotions. Going "all visceral" and not factual in an interview is a sure way to plummet your odds of success.

All the information you just gathered serves as your background information to set the stage for your strategy. While you might not use this information in conversation, it will help you model your optimum strategy for producing results. It will help you discover what they want out of you and it will help you model your strategy and wording regarding how to sell yourself.

Having precise information about the company and the environment in which the company operates will allow you to create an accurate internal framework within which you will navigate your negotiation. Keep these notes and answers safe; these are the building blocks to form your strategy.

"Don't be intimidated by what you don't know. That can be your greatest strength and ensure that you do things differently from everyone else." —Sara Blakely

Statistics Time

Interestingly, HR employs the most amount of women compared to any other job sector. It's deciding whether this is a positive or negative that causes much debate.

Do we want to be pigeon-holed... Should we be grateful?

- Over 73% of managerial jobs in HR are held by women
- Over 82 % of all administrative jobs in HR are now held by women

Source: Bureau of Labor Statistics 2015

Chapter 3

THE COMMON FOUR

We can ignore reality, but we cannot ignore the consequences of ignoring reality. —Ayn Rand

It was 2 p.m. on my average day, listening to the third phone call from a distressed woman, unhappy with the way she was being paid (rather, what she was not being paid). As I listened, it dawned on me after all these conversations, a pattern was emerging! In all the stories and scenarios women were coming to the Salary Coaching Team for help, they seemed to fall into four common situations.

The common four are not ground-breaking realizations. They are real life experiences and most of you will probably be able to take a look at your own circumstance and relate to at least one of them.

Let's not look at being part of the common four as a negative. Instead, let's see this as the realization of your situation, that start of your journey to forming your own strategy and realizing your worth. It should be liberating, exciting; embrace it!

In sharing a few of my clients personal stories and how their situations fit into the common four, I challenge you to see if you can relate to one of these stories and ask yourself, "Are you playing the lead role in one of The Common Four?"

The Common Four

1. Not knowing what you are worth and being misinformed

$125k should be $300k! My client could not believe this was her market value. As a top graduate training for her residency, Rosie was frustrated, annoyed, and ticked off when she called me. A few months before our call, she had found out she was the lowest paid throughout her entire residency.

At the start of her residency, Rosie did not know her worth and did not negotiate even though she was effectively the most qualified. After finding out she could have negotiated, she felt she had let herself down.

Determined not to go through the same scenario again after applying for future jobs, she called me for help. She was very clear on her objective in her next role: "I want to make sure I earn at least $125k. After all, I am a highly trained doctor and six figures sounds about right." She had carried out some web research and felt the figure to be realistic for her position. Rosie also knew of preferred practices she wanted to apply to; and she knew what her ideal company and position looked like.

Naturally, I questioned the web research and carried out my own detailed market analysis for the position she was looking at. It became apparent that every practice she was looking to apply to was not only different in size and location, but their values on salary were very different.

An important interlude here: Most of the research we are able to do as individuals (even if we dig deep) is still different from what we do at Salary Coaching for Women. What a cursory online research will likely show is employee-reported data (that means data reported by individuals who have held the job, rather than by the company who hires for the job). Companies rarely choose to rely on this type of data since there is an incentive for individuals to misrepresent their salaries when reporting them. Instead, companies prefer to safeguard their compensation methodologies by paying thousands of dollars a year in order to access company-reported salary surveys (reported by other peer companies in the same industry). This data is highly guarded by the surveying company; it's what keeps the survey company in business after all. Thus, as individuals, we can't find any of it in our own Google search. But at Salary Coaching, we buy this data to help our clients, and our mission is to close the gender wage gap even if you can't afford our services. Keep reading this book so that you can learn to maximize the power of free available data: how to look for it and how to use it.

Rosie needed to know her worth rather than focus on what salary she wanted to achieve. In looking at our survey data, and narrowing down what type of practice she wanted to work with, and which two locations she particularly wanted to move to, we soon found she could earn $250k. This was her market value. Rosie was dumbfounded. After all, she thought she was aiming high at $125k.

"How on earth do I ask for that salary?" Rosie asked.

"You don't," I replied. "When they ask you how much you want to earn, you slyly deflect it. Respond by saying something along the lines of, 'I appreciate you asking that question, and I could really use your help in answering it. I am in the process of talking to a couple of practices right now and since I'm fresh out of residency, I could really use your help and insight into how you would value someone with my background and skill sets."

All of a sudden the tables are turned. Rosie did not throw

a random number or her $125k to them, but made a polite confrontation without antagonizing anyone. She was asking for their input, therefore showing that she trusted their assessment. The practice reviewed the position, market, and assessed her worth. They came back to her with an offer of $300k. Rosie could not believe the figure offered and the simple way she achieved it. No long, drawn-out negotiation or mind games. She was just simply aware of her worth in the market and was not afraid to form a strategy and follow it.

In the wise words of Pitbull, "Ask for money, you get advice, ask for advice, get money twice."

Rosie actually had her heart set on another practice in another state. Knowing her worth, she applied the same strategy. This time, when they asked her what salary she was looking for, she confirmed she had an outstanding offer of $300k. The practice decided to match the offer and offer her ten additional vacation days a year!

By virtue of being informed and knowing how to ask, Rosie was able to find out her worth directly from the horse's mouth and use it to her advantage.

---

2. Fear of rejection

Sitting there, staring at the clock she had just been given for her long-standing service with the company, it suddenly dawned on Abbie that she needed to wake up and realize that this symbolic gift was as good as it was going to get. She had never spoken up for herself because she feared losing her job; she assumed her loyalty would pay off. But today, she realized she needed (and owed it to herself) to advocate for her career, or the next fifteen years would mirror the last fifteen.

For fifteen years, Abbie worked as an HR Administrator. She had never received a promotion or significant raise other than an ocassional bonus, or the annual cost of living increase the company gave as standard for all employees.

Fifteen years ago, her starting salary had been $34k and today, it was merely $42k. Her role had evolved over the years, but her compensation had not. The company had tripled in size, technology had evolved, she had been instrumental in implementing and maintaining the new systems, and all she had to show for it was a clock.

Abbie had spent all that time waiting for the recognition or pay rise she was convinced would head her way. Each time she was given a new responsibility, she was sure this time would be when the raise would come. Of course, it never did.

The clock made Abbie wake up to the reality and disappointment she had felt for so long, and she called us for help. Until this point, the fear of rejection had held her back—not knowing what would happen if she approached her employer or even how to talk to them. She carried on in her role feeling increasingly demotivated and frustrated.

The first thing we did was review her job role. After fifteen years working for a company that consistently added new responsibilities, I was convinced the job role was nothing like the job she was now carrying out for the company.

It turns out the job responsibilities she was currently carrying out had changed by 90%; and Abbie was astounded by this harsh reality. She was responsible for managing the compensation within the company, dealt with employee retention issues, and was the main HR company contact for over 200 employees. Abbie was no longer an HR Administrator; she was running HR.

How had this been going on for so long? In this circumstance, the company did not carry out appraisals or review positions.

Like many companies, it fell into the habit of assuming employees would bring it up themselves, or in this case, just keep quiet.

After reviewing her job description and forming a new one to include all of her current responsibilities, we contacted local companies and asked what they would be willing to pay for someone in the same position. We looked at (paid) survey data. We also asked companies based on her new job description what her title should be. Each company confirmed Abbie was indeed an HR Manager and could easily command a salary of at least $65k.

As with most of the clients we work with, when the market data comes back and they realize the salary they could and should be paid, the shock creates anger and frustration that they had not acted sooner. Once we formed a strategy for Abbie to approach her employer, she gained enough confidence to march in and get what she deserved (real time market data is a sure way of supplying facts that cannot be ignored...). Abbie walked away from the meeting with $65k... A much better reward for fifteen years of loyal service.

---

3. The impostor's dilemma

> I have written eleven books, but each time I think, 'Uh oh, they're going to find out now. I've run a game on everybody, and they're going to find me out. —Maya Angelou

No matter who you are or where you come from, we are often hit with a sudden feeling of self-doubt. **When it comes to the workplace, self-doubt can have a devastating effect and sabotage our ability to move forward with our careers.**

More often than not, women seem to exhibit more self-doubt than men. In part, men have an assertiveness to them that tends to carry them through their lives and their careers without the worry or feelings of self-doubt that can strongly haunt women. Today, evolutionary psychology has pretty much demolished the blank-slate theory of gender differences. We now know that male and female brains are subtly different, and that these differences (along with hormones) have powerful influences on personality and behavior. This is not to say that some men don't exhibit the same traits as women and vice-versa, but proportionally speaking, what I've found in the world of salary negotiation supports the hypothesis of gender differences. Self-doubt being one of these differences, we cannot help but have our work cut out for us. It's part of us.[1] However, that does not mean it cannot be questioned and dealt with.

Interestingly enough, when a man sees a job posting, if he feels he can perform 60% of the requirements in the job description, he will apply for the job with confidence. Women, on the other hand, rarely apply unless they confidently hit at least 90% of the requirements in the job description.

The effects this self-doubt can have on home life and our health are even more distressing. Heart disease is still the number one killer of women in the western world. Many studies [2] prove that the permanent state of anxiety and stress we suffer through managing our careers, home life, and self-doubt, are the biggest contributing factors to heart disease. Stay-at-home women are not exempt from this; depression and stress caused by the feeling they

1. Curious about whether this is socially or genetically ingrained? Check out Moheb Costandi's "50 Human Brain Ideas You Really Need to Know"

2. Quick article: https://www.cardiosmart.org/News-and-Events/2016/03/Anxiety-Masks-Heart-Disease-in-Women; Long read: American Heart Association journal circulation: Cardiovascular Quality and Outcomes; Factsheet from the CDC: http://www.cdc.gov/dhdsp/data_statistics/fact_sheets/fs_women_heart.htm

are not being compensated or rewarded for their work plays a big factor in increased risk of heart disease.

The same study in men found that, when in stressful senior positions, their stress levels dropped quite dramatically after clocking out at 5 p.m., and by the time they reached home, the levels were down and manageable.

Women in the same positions, however, saw unchanging stress levels even after clocking out, especially those who had to go home and take care of the kids, cook, clean, and think about the tasks for the next day. In some cases, stress levels increased. This is living in a state of permanent high stress and anxiety, and it makes our bodies vulnerable to disease. This is a scary reality of the modern world.

When it comes to the impostor's dilemma, check out another example:

Nancy had been in her job for fifteen years. In that time, her salary had increased from $39k to $47k and her job description was barely recognizable. Nancy got few, small increases, and no title promotion. Nancy realized this could no longer go on. She had reached her limit of patience and hated her job. Something had to change, and she needed the recognition and pay rise she knew she deserved.

When I heard from Nancy, the first thing she said was, "I hate my job, I get no recognition." Another case of a woman in despair over the way she was being treated, and allowing herself to be treated! I went through the usual process and questioned Nancy. It was clear she was essentially doing the work of a lawyer. As a paralegal at a large non-profit, her role involved managing money received from donors, ensuring all funds were regulated and met with the necessary legal compliance. She was only supposed to prepare the necessary documents for the lawyer to research and analyze, but over the years, she was the one who had become the expert in compliance. The lawyer merely signed off on her work, rarely taking the time to even review it. Nancy was more familiar with the vast number of tax codes and compliance regulations across multiple states than anyone else in the organization.

On top of that, Nancy realized there were a lot of funds that could not be used because of legal limitations or obsolete directives. She pioneered the methodologies to take the funds to court and implement them so the organization could appropriate the funds. She saved the organization a huge amount of money and recaptured donations/funds previously lost in the system. This should have been the work of a fully qualified lawyer.

Remembering her statement when we first spoke about hating her job, it actually became clear she loved the job, but knew she was never going to be recognized, and that it would be a HUGE uphill battle. She had asked for a raise on multiple occasions, but never got it. Nancy felt like (and was made to feel like) an impostor, questioning herself and not believing her own self-worth. Nancy felt helpless, bitter, under-qualified, and lost because she had no leverage.

"Maybe this is all I am going to get," she said to me. "If this is all you are willing to believe you are worth, I dare say that indeed you are done. But if you are willing to do the work to generate leverage on your behalf, you will create other opportunities for yourself," I responded. With that, we kicked into gear and started figuring out her worth.

"To hell with circumstances, I create my own opportunities." – Bruce Lee

We reached out to over ten organizations within the same sector. As it happened, the system she had created did not exist within similar non profits, but they could benefit from it. The system meant organizations would save time and resources trying to recapture lost funds, therefore increasing overall efficiency; it really was a breakthrough system. When Nancy realized the significance of what she had pioneered, it dawned on her that she was not confined to her current circumstances.

The end result? Many companies come back and said they'd love to have a role like this and would be prepared to pay in the region of $79k. When one company heard someone like Nancy existed, they made her an instant offer of $90k! In this example, Nancy finally realized she was not an impostor, that her employer was never going to recognize her worth, and when you have to move, you move!

This is an astoundingly common issue; do you recognize yourself in it?

Here's another one: When I met Leanne, she was a professor of neurology who had just come to the end of her current contract, and the department had confirmed they would not renew it. This created a huge amount of self-doubt for Leanne—she was under the impression that her contract would be renewed because of her good work.

She was entering the job market feeling very insecure about her chances. She had always really wanted to apply for a tenured position in academia, but felt that her pedigree had diminished because of what she interpreted as rejection. This is when she turned to me for help.

We worked heavily on rewiring her mentality of being a fraud. In spite of her doubts, we helped her find and apply for other academic roles across the country. We came across the perfect job for her in California. Her worst fear was how to respond in an interview to why her contract wasn't renewed. We rehearsed this question at least twenty times and refocused it by simply anchoring her response to the differences between the department's current research needs relative to her specific focus.

In other words, we took the blame off her shoulders and put it squarely where it belonged.

The funny thing about this story... California never asked the dreaded question, but they did offer her a tenure track role.

-----

4. Negotiation from anger and emotion rather than rational thinking

It started on a Tuesday morning with a very angry phone call from a woman named Rita. She called me after finding out she was being paid half of what she was worth. Her salary was $110k, but her job role was commanding at least $230k a mere hundred miles away.

Rita was setting the strategy and was the director of her division, but she was being low-balled as she had started at the company as a researcher. As the company grew, her role grew, but this was not recognized in terms of pay. While unintentionally (for some), many companies end up paying less for internal talent that moves up the ranks when compared to what they would pay to acquire new talent.

When she approached the company for a raise and recognition of the increase in her responsibilities, they said because her area was so specialized and they were still a relatively new company, they required funding from government and could not warrant a rise in her salary.

Part of her division did involve work relating to government contracts but half did not. HR said that, since they were not guaranteed funding from the government, they could not increase her salary and that they were under no obligation to give her a raise.

Just to rub salt in her wounds, Rita was at the coffee machine one morning and overheard a colleague mention he was getting a bonus of 10%. She asked him what this meant in monetary value and he told her! He was a peer level director with very similar responsibilities including the government split projects, he was on $200k, AND he was going to get a raise again this year.

Rita was furious, crying, shaking and just wanted to quit then and there. At this point, though, Rita's friend told her to call me before she went to HR. Thankfully, she did.

I was aware of a salary survey used in her highly specialized industry. This survey was widely acclaimed and known for their accurate and credible information. It's also extremely difficult for individuals to get a hold of this information, as they will only sell it to "relevant" companies (in other words, they are very secretive about their content—if you are not in the industry, they will not sell it to you).

Through my many contacts, I was able to access the data and we prepared her case. I had a gut feeling we could generate leverage. I suggested we reach out to other peer companies in the same sector and brainstorm who, if she could choose, she would like to work with.

From reaching out, Rita actually received verbal offers from two other companies. We simply contacted other companies and explained she was looking to renegotiate her position. What does her job role look like in your company and how would you value someone like her? It was clear from this research and from the industry-specific survey, Rita was worth $200 – $250k.

A brief interlude: When you market price a position, you look at where the person is in terms of proficiency relative to their role. If someone in a role has a particularly long learning curve ahead, they are likely to be priced at or below the 50th percentile of the market (though this may also depend on company policy). Generally, when someone is priced at the 50th percentile of the market, it means that the person is proficient and, if they were to start the job today, they would hit the ground running. Someone who would not only hit the ground running but also be able to set the strategic direction of their role, might command upwards of the 75th percentile of their relevant market in terms of salary. More of this number crunching in a few chapters.

Rita took this information to the boss in charge and it turned out he was desperate to keep her. Using her leverage and credible information, Rita asked for $240k and wanted to work from home three days a week. Her boss had to follow bureaucratic loops, taking the request to HR who flatly refused to negotiate, but Rita knew what she was worth and was prepared to walk away.

She took her time and thought through her emotions. In the end, she accepted an offer with another company in another city, a company that offered $235 (well within her goal) along with flexibility of working remotely two days a week, and a company she had highlighted when we carried out our market research.

I see this scenario all too often. **When you find your value, when you can see clearly the difference between what you earn and what you should be earning, you no longer lack the confidence to be held back.** Many women move on to greener pastures even though that was not their initial intention.

So many women do not realize there are opportunities out there, opportunities that might not be obvious in the beginning, but ones that will open so many doors for them if they look hard enough. Sometimes you might not be able to see past the thick cloud of self-doubt... but keep reaching. My clients have proved it every day and, where there's a will, there's a way.

Take the time to step back from your situation, form your strategy, and review your options. Reach out to other companies you are interested in and say, "Listen, can I talk to you?" Ask for their ADVICE and feedback. The key at this stage is to listen, drink it in, and ask the right questions.

So what are the questions you need to ask and how do you

ask them? Time for a little homework—grab your pen and notepad and answer the following questions.

1. How much do you think you are worth?
2. What has been one of your biggest failures in life?
3. How did you bounce back?
4. What role do YOU have in your own success?

Statistics Time

"The US wage gap is getting worse."

This was a leading headline in a November 18th, 2015 report from CNN Money. And if we reverse course, we will have to sit patiently and wait until 2133 before we can start to be paid the same as men. Yep, that is how long they believe the gap will take to close: 118 years.

CNN also published a survey listing the number of days per year women worked for "free," based on earnings spread over 365 days:

- France – 183 days
- Germany – 154 days
- Canada – 139 days
- USA – 133 days
- China/Japan – 128 days
- UK – 125 days

The same survey also found there is not one country in the entire world where women are paid the same as men. Can you wait 118 years to be paid what you deserve?

Chapter 4

INTERNAL RETROSPECTION

He who asks a question remains a fool for five minutes,
he who does not ask a question remains a fool forever.
—Chinese Proverb

Mirror, mirror on the wall...

Be forewarned, this chapter will make your head spin with questions. But in a good way!

"Knowledge is having the right answer, intelligence is asking the right question."

Our lives are full of little questions. What should I wear today, what should I have for breakfast, what route should I take to work, what do I pack for lunch? It never ends. Our brain is constantly firing and trying to answer small questions by making small decisions. It's no wonder that we never really have the time or the opportunity to sit and ask ourselves big life and career questions.

When you really think about your career and what your goals are, it can suddenly have a startling impact on how you view yourself within your current situation. You may suddenly question if you are in the right career, it may make you realize you want to focus on working less hours to be with your family, or you may feel empowered to find out your worth and start forming the strategy to obtain it.

If you could do anything in this world and be passionate about it, what would you do? There are no expectations and there are no right or wrong answers. The first female president of the United States? An astronaut? A sheep herder in New Zealand? Be sincere. Write down the answer to this question and keep it safe!

However—if we are asked what our personal goals are, the question all of a sudden takes on a different meaning. Goals feel more concrete, scarier, and a little more serious.

For the most part, we care what society think of us, we want to be accepted, liked, and feel part of the crowd—whatever your crowd may be! So when we really ask ourselves the question of what our personal goals are, we often answer with what our goals should be from the socially acceptable lens rather than our own. Answering it truthfully will feel uncomfortable because it's not something we are used to doing, and might even feel a little selfish.

Many of the people we help at Salary Coaching feel this way when asked to answer the personal goals question. They assume their goal is to earn a lot of money, to be at a higher level within their company. But your answers should be even more selfish than money and status, it's time to think about YOU and what you want from your career. These goals should be so personal that no one can take them away from you once achieved. I'm talking about fulfilling your most innate desires. Do you want to be rich or do you want to be fulfilled by what you do? Do you want to be in a position of power, or would you rather be passionate about what you do? Figuring out those goals that lie deep inside you can be a cathartic and pivotal moment in your career and life as a whole.

Answering a few of these questions will help you realize what

YOU want out of your career and stop you from being yet another unhappy career ladder junkie. We are often led to make a decision from emotion and anxiety, but when you dig deep and answer the 'what do I want' question, you will know where you stand and you will know exactly where you are headed. You'll be proud and you will feel empowered, liberated, and strong. The best part of knowing your true goals: NOBODY CAN TAKE THEM AWAY FROM YOU.

The world will need to be ready for you.

Coaching Tips

Get a pen and paper and answer these questions. Remember this is no wrong or right answer, and note down exactly what your gut instinct tells you.

1. What are your immediate career goals?
2. What would be your ideal lifestyle?
3. What do you love about your work?
4. What do you hate about your work?
5. Where do you see yourself retiring from?
6. What are your hobbies?
7. If you could do anything in this world and be passionate about it, what would you do?
8. Now the biggie: What are your personal goals?

This chapter is meant to prepare you mentally; the next few chapters will hopefully give you skills, knowledge, and belief that you can achieve what you want from your career and realize your worth.

Statistics Time

According to the 2015 edition of The Conference Board Job

Satisfaction survey, only half of US workers (49.6 percent) are satisfied with their jobs.

Chapter 5

GET MORE BUCK FOR YOUR BANG

When you realize how much you are worth, you will stop giving people discounts. —Unknown

Answering the questions from Chapter Four will put you in a good frame of mind to continue on your journey to figure out what you're worth.

We are often working in jobs where we just accept what we are paid because we trust that the people setting our salaries will stay on top of our compensation throughout our stay at that organization. Surely they know what the market is dictating and making sure we are being fairly paid?

Well, that's putting a lot of trust in people, people who are ultimately there to make money off of our work. After all, that's business right?!

We want and expect our superiors to be proactive in managing us, reward us for hard work, and promote us when we go above and beyond their expectations. But unfortunately in today's society and particularly in competitive workplace environments, this is hardly the case. Managers are so overburdened with responsibilities and meeting the bottom line, they hardly have time to look out for their own careers, let alone cultivate that of others.

In the tornado of everyday work and stress, managers often find themselves short of time and resources to manage the satisfaction of their most valuable assets: employees. You have to take charge to make sure you are making what you deserve.

Patience is a virtue

Figuring out your worth is the first step to becoming more empowered, knowledgeable, strategic, and ultimately confident enough to negotiate and get paid what you deserve, based only on your skills and position. It's akin to laying a solid foundation for a house. You'll be ready to craft your strategy to tackle asking your busy boss for that raise. If you know your worth, you become unshakeable.

Employed but not empowered

As an employee, you are accountable for upholding the organization's rules and expectations. You are working for a business, a business that exists to make money and remain profitable.

Are you in a position where you enjoy your role, but you feel you are not being paid your worth, or are you working in a job you've come to hate because of the long hours and increased responsibilities? Has "going the extra mile" come to be expected of you, but it goes unappreciated?

If any of these scenarios resonate, you are not alone.

"People work for money, but go the extra mile for recognition, praise, and rewards." —Dale Carnegie

In 2014, a well researched article by Jeff Fermin at www.officevibe.com listing 10 Shocking Stats About Disengaged

Employees went viral across the globe because it highlighted just how bad employee engagement is today. Here are a few stats:

- 70% of US workers are not engaged.
- 89% of employers think employees leave for money, 12% of employees actually leave for money.
- 75% of people voluntarily leaving their jobs, don't quit their jobs, they quit their bosses.

Look for the right job role

What is the right job role for you? This is a question most of us take years to answer. You have to kiss a few job role frogs before you find your job role prince, and that's totally normal.

Looking for the right job role can be just as demotivating as being in a job you are unhappy with. Reaching out and facing potential rejection might fill you with fear, especially if you are just getting back into work after having a family (see Danielle's example later in the chapter). Getting your career back can feel like an uphill battle, and self-doubt along with not knowing the current market can leave you in the dark. But read on to see how to get the job role you want, with the pay you want.

"The secret of change is to focus all of your energy, not on fighting the old, but on building the new." —Socrates from *The Way of The Peaceful Warrior*

Becoming Sherlock Holmes

This is where you turn detective for the sake of figuring out your worth. Now is time to take another opportunity to review your current situation, and where you ultimately want to be. Follow these action points in order to craft your strategy, in order to know what you're worth and how to ask for it.

- Research, research, research.

Gathering evidence will be a big part of ensuring you are knowledgeable about your position and skills. Knowledge will make your negotiation strategy stronger.

The secret most people never find out about compensation, is that setting a salary is not a true science. Much of it is art! It is within the artistic component that you will always find room to negotiate. As long as you teach yourself how to ask for it, you can aim higher. As I've said before, it is a matter of perception. What this means for you, is that if you can make a compelling case as to why you should earn what you say you should earn, you can get them to agree to it.

- Reach out to an acquaintance, cold call or email someone within HR, or preferably the compensation function, for a similar organization and be completely forthcoming. Ask them, "What would you pay someone in this position?" Or if that feels too straight forward, "I'm doing some personal research for this type of position. Can you tell me more about this role at your company?"

Even if they don't give you a straightforward answer, you might obtain a salary range from them or guidance as to how to obtain their salary range. You could also probably find it on their website. The worst case is that they just won't give you any information, which is no different from where you are now. The best case is that they won't only give you a range, but they'll tell you that they applaud your diligence and say they are interested in hiring you if an opening arises for that position.

For the most part, they will likely be happy to share this information. If they are not, ask them to guide you in the right direction. Call as many organizations as you can and start to build a salary picture. Here is an example call-script of what I would say:

"Hi, my name is Olivia. I am an Administrative Assistant at XYZ Company and I'm trying to figure out what my market value is in order for me to talk to my boss about a raise. I realize this is an unconventional call, but would there be any way that you could provide me with information to help me figure out what I am worth?

If they say NO:

Ok, I completely understand. Would it be possible for you to share a salary range for this type of role with me?

If they say NO:

I totally understand it. On a more personal note, as someone who works in HR/Compensation, could I get your advice and guidance as to how I might best find an appropriate reflection of what my salary could be? I'm feeling a little underpaid at my current job, so I'm trying to figure out my worth. I might add that my current salary is $45,000.

I sincerely thank you for any help or guidance you could give me."

Everyone likes pontificating and giving advice. Sit back and listen to all the clues they give you. If you choose to email organizations instead, enclose your current position description as well as a highly polished résumé (Don't worry, the résumé section is coming up).

- Research the company you are working for/want to work for.

How have they rewarded colleagues before? What is the policy on salary raises? Who will you be negotiating with? How do they like to see evidence presented? Is the organization as a whole known for being bureaucratic? Or is it a more collegial environment? Have they been in the media lately? If so, why? Gaining insight into your company will make sure you fully understand their stance on negotiation.

- Know your job.

Sounds obvious right? You will be surprised at the amount of women who come to me and have a job description that has no relation to the role they are currently fulfilling. And it's suprisingly often that I come across cover letters and résumés that in no way mirror the needs of the position description in question. If you do not know what is expected of you, how can you be valued?

- Map out your strengths.

Think objectively for a few moments... What are you bad at?

Ok, now that that's out of the way, how about, what are you good at? What do people like about you?

When being complimented, we are often told "you always" or "you are known for" and we take no notice of what these words are actually telling us:

"You always give the best ideas in meetings."

"You are known for giving the best sales presentations."

These are actually achievements—we are being told, but we just don't hear it.

The strategy we need to develop from this is, when you are asked about your weaknesses, how do you wrap a narrative around it so that you end up talking about your strengths. Take the comments you may have heard and make a list, is there a pattern? Our strongest attributes will often make repeat appearances.

Meet Danielle – A mom with many strengths!

Danielle was a military wife who had spent the last twenty years homeschooling and taking care of her four kids. But, when it came time for her husband to retire after 20 years of service, she wanted to reintegrate herself into the workforce. Yet entering the workforce after taking such a long break was daunting for her, so she turned to me for help.

Because my husband also served in the military, I have had the great fortune of helping quite a few military wives reintegrate into the workforce. What I have found is that military spouses in particular seem to have a hard time thinking they are worth much in the workforce after trying to reintegrate from a long hiatus. Yet much of this is really a matter of perception: it all comes down to how you portray and perceive your experience. If you think it doesn't add value, you are right, and if you think it does add value, you are also right.

We spent time going through her résumé and polishing up her huge number of skills and highlighted the strengths developed by so many years of homeschooling kids. She had to be organized, self-sufficient, manage the expectations of learning from her kids, create and manage several schedules, and be a master of staying on top of things.

Danielle also had an impressive array of volunteer experience, including being involved at a high level with Red Cross where she organized volunteers on site for disasters like Hurricane Katrina.

She decided to apply for a role managing a team at a regional bakery and, because we reinvented her résumé to highlight the things she had honed from homeschooling her kids and running a household while her husband was deployed, she was viewed as the ideal candidate and got the job, even without traditional team management experience at another business.

In Her Own Words

If Danielle's story doesn't convince the nay-saying side of your brain that you can learn your worth and how to ask for it, here's a letter from a client *(which arrived accompanied by a decadent bottle of 2002 wine!)*. She needed to figure out exactly what was expected of her within her current role and, in doing so, we found out she could also use this to negotiate better hours and a salary raise. She had never negotiated a salary before.

Hi Oli,

The hour you spent talking with me was really helpful. I was able to get my salary from $85k to $95k and a bit of stock options. In addition, I was able to get more paid time off, which is going to be a huge help for me and my family. Talking with you put my offering into perspective and allowed me to negotiate confidently.

Thank you for lending your expertise. It made a big difference in my FIRST salary negotiation.

I hope you enjoy the wine.

Sincerely,

Jessica

Alright Sherlock, back to your detective work. The next action point is a biggie.

- Write a killer résumé.

Your résumé

Make sure to check at the door everything you've ever learned about résumés. We are about to blow up conventional wisdom on résumé preparation. My advice is coming from a very different angle than what you will hear from recruiters and career counselors/coaches.

And here's why you need to listen to my advice: One of the reasons people from all over the US and Latin America ask me to help with their résumés is because I've been coveted (and hated) for putting price tags on people when hired. I spent the better part of a decade setting price tags on résumés and people on behalf of multiple organizations. I've seen what works and what doesn't. I've been the one "behind the scenes" telling hiring managers what they can and cannot pay for someone. And here's another little compensation secret: the person who comes up with the salary range will likely not be part of the interviewing process. They will judge you on your résumé and cover letter (or just your resume) relative to the position description.

Being a data-driven person, I've kept track of the winning patterns—and losing ones. This has earned me accolades like being considered one of the top résumé experts in the country (by recruiter.com), along with landing me opportunities to share my advice at international conferences, universities, and in countless magazines, newspapers, and online articles (for updated media publications, go to www.salarycoaching.com).

Writing a résumé is a healthy way of keeping up to date with your job description and staying in tune with a skill most struggle to perfect. A killer résumé will put you to the top of the pile. The next few steps have nothing to do with formatting or what type of paper you should use to print your résumé. My mission is to help you maximize the use of content in order to achieve a) being put at the top of the pile and b) maximizing the potential salary offer you will receive.

First Résumé Rule: Don't be a copy cat... but be aware that imitation is the sincerest form of flattery. Use keywords from the position description, but not whole phrases in your résumé.

Without mimicking the exact language of the position description, make sure that you address all of the pointers in the position description. Usually if the position description has been well vetted and thought out by the company, you will find that the accountabilities of the position are listed in order of importance.

If the first accountability is snow plowing, that means that the primary role of importance within this job will likely be snow plowing.

If the last accountability is sweeping, that means that it will be part of your job but not as important as snow plowing. Use this information strategically and you will crack your résumé. Make sense?!

Second Résumé Rule: Read their minds and tell them what they want to hear.... Be the solution to their problems.

Use your past experience to hone in on the things the person hiring wants to hear. In your résumé, if you have experience in plowing and sweeping, make sure to address these accountabilities in a way that makes the hiring manager say, "Hey, that's totally like what we do here," rather than saying, "This person totally just copy and pasted the position description into her résumé," or worse, "They didn't even read the job description."

At the end of the day, all the formatting in the world can't save you from the bottom of the pile if you can't add value to the quandary of the person hiring (hence they are hiring!).

Third Résumé Rule: Can the canned language.

"Strong work ethic and interpersonal skills. Excellent written, verbal, and interpersonal skills. Organized and efficient. Effective as a leader, excellent skills organizing and motivating people. Commitment to diversity. Works well in a team or independently."

I cannot tell you the amount of times I have read the exact same words on thousands of résumés. At this point, you get pushed down and lost in the pile of suckers who said the same thing as you!

It is important to realize that your résumé is supposed to reflect the best YOU on paper relative to the position you are interviewing for. Canned language inevitably comes across as insincere. You've probably heard varied opinions about tenses, language, and the use of "I" in your resume. None of these matter if you are not persuasive and engaging.

Essentially, when it comes down to it, what really matters is how you frame your experience and what you highlight. You need to highlight the background that is most relevant to the potential employer. Simply ask yourself, "How can I add value to this job?"

I'm not here to tell you what your resume needs to look like. I have literally set the salary for THOUSANDS of résumés and I can guarantee you that there is no standard format that will likely get you hired more so than any other format. There are standards that you can use as guides in specific industries such as IT, Healthcare, etc. But at its core, the deciding factor in whether or not you even make it to the salary setting stage will be if you are liked by the hiring manager.

Statistical Interlude: It will take your interviewer less than 10 minutes to assess whether they like you or not. The interviewer will spend the rest of the interview finding ways to corroborate their assessment of "yay" or "nay."

So I will leave it up to you to decide what template, format, and tense best suits your résumé. If you've done your research properly, you will know if you should keep it formal or if you can get away with being lax. I once set a salary for a guy who was unemployed, but nonetheless listed his "Current job" to read something along these lines:

Lawn Gnome Officer (2013-current):

- I sit on my front porch and stare at my lawn gnomes on a daily basis, ensuring they don't run away.
- If needed, I run after them ensuring they stay confined in my garden.
- When household items such as remote controls, cell phones, or shoes disappear, I promptly interrogate them and search their surroundings.
- Project in progress: I am currently spearheading a sophisticated sting operation in the laundry room to catch Lawn Gnomes that apparently enjoy stealing single socks.

Needless to say, this guy got the job because the Hiring Manager simply liked him.

Back to your résumé. At its core, the four most basic components of your résumé are (not necessarily titled as follows): *Summary/Initial Blurb*, *Experience*, *Skills*, and *Education*. Any additional sections might be nice to have, but are not fundamental for every single résumé. I personally like to see an About Me section at the end where your résumé can really come alive by giving me a better picture of who you are, but alas, this is not fundamental. It's about content, not format.

Summary/Initial Blurb: This is the gateway to your résumé. Use this as an entry path to your résumé so that you can subliminally guide the reader to want to hire. This is how you get past the bouncer at the party. Without some initial section of sorts, you are simply flooding the reader with experience information that has no direction. Our brains don't like chaos, which means they will not like you.

The ideal way of thinking about it is as if this initial section were a close friend of the Hiring Manager reading your résumé. This friend has just told the Hiring Manager:

"Seriously, you need to meet this amazing woman who would be ideal for that job! She can work miracles. She is an expert at managing multiple projects and meeting tight deadlines. Her organization skills are impeccable and she is excellent communicator, both verbally and on paper!"

Get it? If your résumé gets read at all, this is the one section that *will* get read by virtue of being at the beginning. Make it count!

Experience: This is where the money is. Literally. If there's any negotiation room within the role, and you meet the skills and requirements for the job, where you land on the salary spectrum will be determined primarily by this section.

This is where the Hiring Manager corroborates what his friend told him (could be a her, but I'm going with him for now) about you. The key is to get him to think: "Wow, this gal could really meet the needs of the job... and maybe exceed our expectations."

How do you sell yourself in this section? With only copying key words (NOT PHRASES), mimic the position description through your experiences. Play chameleon with your own experiences.

Say you've applied to an Admin Assistant role that supports two directors and you've never reported to two folks before. They need someone to work magic with schedules, calls, and keep the two directors organized.

Let's say your last job you were technically the admin for only one director, but the company was fairly small, so you wore many hats. How can you wrap a narrative around this experience that showcases instances where you dealt with competing priorities, maintaining schedules, and keeping cool through it all?

Furthermore, how could you convey through your experience that the person you reported to was left utterly satisfied by your ability to juggle it all? Do you see where we are headed with this? Use your words wisely to assuage the reader. Think from their standing point what it is that they want. Show that you can satisfy their job needs because you can empathize with them and soothe their needs nicely. Sell it, girl!

Skills and Education: This section is pretty straight forward. I prefer education listed above skills, but there's no magic bullet here. This section will only get glanced at, so my one piece of advice is don't waste precious space with irrelevant skills. List in order of relevance relative to the position description. It's great that you are a certified lifeguard, but if you are applying for a Mechanical Engineer position, this is not the place to list that.

A note on About Me sections.

I can't speak for everyone on this one, but when setting salaries, I personally really enjoyed reading these at the end of résumés. In my opinion, they bring the résumé alive and make you whole, they make me remember your name and make me want to meet you. It can be a breath of fresh air after reading and scanning whether you measure up or not.

Lets be honest here, I wouldn't necessarily feel inclined to meet you because you have a long list of skills, a PhD, or studied at an Ivy League. But if you compete in rodeos or you volunteer at your local children's hospital by dressing up like Batman, you become much more intriguing. I think of this section as your final opportunity to hook the reader in with something interesting about you.

Even if your hobbies are not earth-shattering, tell the reader something interesting about it. Say you collect stamps, share a neat fact about them, like you have 10,000 of them, or the oldest one dates to 1919. Which is the rarest one? If you are a recreational runner, tell the reader why you picked up running, what makes you passionate about it, or about how much you raised for that charity run last year.

Your *About Me* section can be your last opportunity to shock and awe the reader. I recommend you include it!

Cover Letters—Self expression, not a sales pitch

Your cover letter should not be an opportunity to further brag about yourself.

A common cover letter error is falling into the trap of talking about and repeating the highlights already covered in your résumé! This is a big mistake.

Why waste valuable words and time repeating what you have already said? I guarantee the person reading will notice and your credibility and cover letter will get slam dunked in the waste bin.

I have always been an avid reader of cover letters, even though you don't usually need to look at them in order to set a salary. I always like to see how people express themselves in the two or three paragraphs they have to showcase themselves. The most successful cover letters by far are the ones that engage the reader. They make the reader think, "Heck yeah, this person totally understands what we are looking for!"

So how do you engage the hiring manager, especially when they have already read a ton of cover letters before yours?

Solve their problem. Slyly address the issues that must be going unresolved as a result of this vacancy and anticipate problems that the hiring manager might be having as a result of the position being unfulfilled. You want him or her to perceive you as not only someone who can fill a role, but someone that they can count on to solve problems and be there as a right hand.

Essentially, you want the reader to finish reading your letter and think, "This is a very thoughtful person; she absolutely understands the environment we operate in and the problems we anticipate here."

Here's a sample winning cover letter:

Dear Joanna,

I hope this email finds you well.

After our last conversation, I did some serious introspection, and realized that perhaps my résumé needed some polishing in order to really reflect my abilities and background relative to the role you are looking to hire.

With the enclosed copy of my résumé, I wish to be considered for the Assistant Director fundraising position.

While on paper my background may be somewhat unconventional, the endorsement letters (also enclosed here) from a broad array of community members might shed some light on the depth of my existing connections with multiple generations of potential donors.

These bonds built by years of trust and friendship will be an immediate asset to maximizing the solicitation efforts for Atlanta Athletics.

Indeed I have barely "scratched the surface" as a volunteer when soliciting my alumni friends to donate funds for the Atlanta Athletics Fund, yet I have been incredibly successful at getting them to participate.

As we have discussed before, I have the innate ability to quickly build rapport and establish trust with people. Be it with individuals or teams (such as the swim teams I coach), being able to empathize and truly listen to what people are saying is a true gift when it comes to getting people to help my causes. I know this will be invaluable when it comes to soliciting large sums for Atlanta Athletics.

Again, I would like to thank you for your encouragement, and if you are available, I would like to meet with you to further discuss this opportunity and get your feedback on my application.

Most sincerely,

Maggie

Did you notice how this letter wasn't written out of the blue to someone that Maggie doesn't know? You should always try to have a conversation with the hiring manager before applying. Review the position description and call to ask any questions or, at the very least, email with questions before you apply.

Reaching out to the company before you even apply will not only ensure that the company is a right fit for you, but it will make you a more coveted applicant if you played your cards right in asking relevant questions the position. Plus, simple name recognition goes a long way.

It's a lot of information to take in and apply when you update and rewrite your résumé, but hey, it isn't supposed to be easy! If actually changing your mindset like this chapter proposes were easy, there would not be any scary statistics like those we have seen throughout the last four chapters.

Following the very simple processes above, however, will aid you and give you the tools you need to negotiate, form your strategy, and empower you to move forward in your career.

You've got this. If you need motivation, just look at these stats....

Statistics Time

Women's earnings by occupation—Below are the top five biggest differences in the wage gender gap by career.

- Financial Managers–Women earn $30k LESS per year

- Credit Counselors and Loan Officers–Women earn $28k LESS per year
- Insurance Sales Agents–Women earn $25k LESS per year
- Property/Real Estate–Women earn $23k LESS per year
- Post Secondary Teachers–Women earn $20k LESS per year

This is for the same job, with the same responsibilities and qualifications.

Source: United States Census Bureau 2015 American community survey – Women's earnings by occupation. Median earnings of full time, year round workers in the past 12 months by sex and occupation.

Chapter 6

THE SECRET

Ssshhhh!

When I say the secret is out, I mean very few people have the luxury of really understanding how the experts work out worth within the market. Suffice it to say, they don't just Google what you should earn and call it a day. It's like going to the grocery store with a list of all the ingredients you need to make an awesome dinner for the family. You fill your basket with all the right ingredients from the list. You leave confident with the knowledge dinner will taste and look like the recipe. Now try shopping without the list and guessing what ingredients you need to make the recipe—dinner will probably end up in the dog's bowl and you will be undoubtedly annoyed.

Knowing your true worth is the defining gender issue of our time, and while legislation can and should be part of the solution, I believe that being knowledgeable about yourself and feeling empowered to make a difference is even more powerful.

Play fair, and share

You may only buy a few cars in your lifetime, but the

people selling you that car have gone through the
process hundreds of times. —Robert Greco

As a compensation expert, worth is at the forefront of everything
I do. Empowering women to find out and realize their worth is
my passion. Sharing my secrets, based on experience and real-
time knowledge, helps women change the way they think about
themselves and their worth. I have every faith it will help you in
your life too.

With this book, take in as much or as little as you want; the
basic principles in the process of finding your worth follow the
same two pillars:

1. Access these tools to create a strong, accurate, and
defensible range of reasons why you are worth what you are
saying. This is for both base salary and bonus opportunities.

2. Make sure you can use your strategy alongside the range
of reasons to be able to confidently negotiate specific to your
personal situation.

Salary Sudoku

In every aspect of our lives, numbers are everything. What
something costs. How many steaks to cook. How many chocolates
to eat. How many chocolates will I SAY I ate? How much to
budget weekly for food. Having enough savings to send our kids
to college. We are hit with numbers and figures every day and
they are even more important when it comes to our
financial health. Let me just set the tone of where we are headed
by starting with percentiles.

Percentiles is a term widely used in business and, rather than
bog you down with crude definitions, let me just give you an easily
digestible example:

Is a 78/90 test score good enough?

You have been studying at night school and you now have to take an end-of-term test to gain your qualification. You are happy to find out that you scored 78 out of 90 on the test.

All the hours of study and stress have paid off, right?!

Well, that figure has no real meaning unless you know what it means relative to others. If everybody else scored 90 and you are the lowest grade in the group, 78 might not be that great. But on the other hand, if at 78 you are the highest score in the class... way to go!

When you are told that your score is in the 90th percentile, that means you scored better than 90% of people who took the test. Got it? Percentile is knowing where you fall within the variables of everyone else.

When it comes to your salary and worth, percentiles are used to put the bounty on you. In business, the percentiles you will fall under are based on the below parameters.

Companies tend to lead or lag the market. In other words, their pay philosophy is to keep up with the top of the market, or to play catch up with salaries as necessary.

In my experience, companies that lead the market will have an easier time retaining top talent. Companies such as Google try paying at 110% of the market. Other companies might not be able to afford or don't want to pay above the 25th percentile (maybe because there is a large supply of potential employees). Keep this in mind when applying for jobs and assessing the company in question.

How you will be slotted into percentiles:

10th to 25th percentile: You are new or fairly new. You might have about a year or more experience; yet you are at entry level for the position.

50th percentile: You have some strong proficiencies and will hit the ground running, but will still have a learning curve.

75th percentile: You are highly qualified and can command this percentile. You will hit the ground running with only a slight learning curve. You will likely contribute to the overall strategy development due to your knowledge and capabilities.

100th percentile: You must be a rockstar. Maybe you should think about taking over your boss's job? Not many companies have a policy of paying at this level... though Google pays at 110%.

While you don't have to fully define where it is that you should be slotted, you need to have a good understanding of where you would fall relative to the position in question.

Ultimately, you need to be *aware* that you will be slotted somewhere in the percentage scale based on:

- The company's pay philosophy
- How qualified you are relative to the position in question.

Understanding this will be fundamental at the negotiation table.

Let's get empowered

Alright, let's get to the nitty gritty of your worth (AKA, let me share my secrets with you).

- Note down your current annual salary.
- What was your final salary at your previous organization?
- Make a list of your salary review dates and how much they were—If any?
- Make a list of bonus payments and how much—If any?
- Note down if bonuses received were based on team results, established metrics, or your own ability to excel at your work.

All of these can be used to speak volumes of your performance. Those tied to your own personal achievements can be an important part of your final negotiation strategy. If you can prove you have achieved your targets, generated a profit, or hit your sales calls, this will help you build a strong case and can be used as a strength when forming your strategy to negotiate.

If you are hitting your targets every month, you know you are good at your job and meeting all the parameters expected of you, you will be classed as being above or significantly above the 50th percentile category and can negotiate your worth based on this.

At this point, once you've got your internal research, I would always recommend you use a professional to use the information you have already gathered and let them carry out the research across the external market. It can get confusing and, frankly, overwhelming. Information is not always accurate and many tend to look at the bigger figures rather than the true figures.

This is where I can help you. At Salary Coaching LLC, we use live market data. In other words, we buy the same surveys used by companies to assess your salary. It would be cost prohibitive for you to buy this data as an individual, but since we help so many women, we can afford to invest thousands of dollars to get current, live data. This guarantees that we can give you an accurate and current, market-based representation of your worth.

All of the sites listed below, albeit less accurate and current, will ask for job title and geographic location. They will give you a broad range of what you are worth within your sector relative to your area. I suggest you look at no less than three sources and compare the data.

Option One: www.salary.com

Option Two: www.indeed.com/salaries

Option Three: www.glassdoor.com/Salaries

Option Four: www.salaryexpert.com/salarycalculator

Using all of the information from these websites will give you a rough idea of your worth. Objectively look at your résumé, your position description and the information you found, then slot yourself within the range of each source (within the 10th and 100th percentile). While not an entirely accurate reflection of the market, you at least get a broader perspective of the numbers you are working with. Look at the whole picture and account for factors such as industry, geography, company size, your background, years of expertise, relevant experience, skills, education, etc. If you were to judge yourself objectively, what percentile would you be in?

Do this for each site and then obtain the average of all the numbers. This will give you a very broad idea of your market worth. You will see what you are being paid relative to others. Can you use any of this information in your strategy and for your negotiation? Remember, if you get overwhelmed (or just want us to do it for you) there is a team of coaches ready to help you.

Puzzle it all together

Carrying out each of the above steps along with your research in previous chapters will now have given you a fairly good idea of what you are worth, how to form your strategy, and you will have a better idea of how to negotiate to get what you deserve.

I can't emphasize enough how important it is that you know your worth. After all, there's no point of leaning in to negotiate if you don't know exactly what you are asking for. Simply going to your boss and asking for a raise with no understanding of your worth is a sure way to get low-balled, or worse, get nothing at all.

Do you have 118 years to close the wage gender pay gap? No?

Me neither! Let's get to work.

Non-Statistics Time (We'll give your brain a little breathing room here...)

Non-monetary perks you can include in negotiations:

- Ask for your compensation and position description to be re-evaluated next quarter
- A change in title
- Assistance with continued education (need an MBA or Certificate to advance your career?)
- Be assigned to a big project or client
- Being paired up with a company mentor to help you gain more experience (and future leverage!)
- Exposure to an area of the company so that you can expand your experience (always wanted to learn about marketing?)
- Flexible work schedule
- More vacation time

Chapter 7

HUDDLE 'ROUND FOR TEAM TALK

When the student is ready, the master appears.
-Buddhist Proverb
Everybody has talent and it's just a matter of
moving around until you've discovered what it is.
-George Lucas

You have reached the chapter where it's my turn to do some of the work: coach you into the next steps to form your strategy.

We have gone through examples, you have asked yourself some important questions, and you hopefully understand exactly why it's important to know your worth. Some of this will be repetitive, but that's the point! You need to continuously ask yourself certain questions and be sure you understand them before moving forward. It's okay to not know the answers to all the questions—that's the wonderful thing about self-development.

Yes, Coach!

Coaching can be described in many ways. For some it's a form of career guidance, encouragement, or development of self-awareness. **But my style of coaching is to empower women first and foremost. That said, empowerment alone won't pay the bills.** In the case of salary negotiation, I believe it's fundamental that empowerment be substantiated by data and irrefutable numbers. I have found that if you don't have an accurate picture of your worth and value, even if you are incredibly empowered when you go talk to your boss, the minute you receive pushback, you will be completely deflated.

I am also a passionate believer in situational awareness, the ability to read what is going on around you and pay attention to your own behavior within your work life. If you are able to read a situation unfolding in front of you, you can be prepared, and this takes the element of emotional responses (instead of confident, rational responses) out of the equation entirely. It's a powerful tool.

You need to be able to back up your actions. This is fundamental because, in the world of business, it's about the bottom line, not your feelings. Sometimes the tide is in your favor and sometimes it's not. My goal is to help you become resilient and help you perceive things with a broader perspective when you're in them. My coaching will help you figure out how to step back and observe your situation objectively in order for you to get what you want.

Time to Assess Yourself

You step into my office or meet me for coffee and I will asses your personal situation. I want you to realize your true value and acknowledge what the strengths and weaknesses are, objectively speaking.

Women generally undervalue themselves even if they know how valuable they are, because we struggle to effectively self-promote ourselves. We are our biggest critics and yes, society can be held *at least* partially responsible for this. But that does not mean we are personally without blame.

In our society, for a man to 'self praise' and 'self promote' results in unquestioned confidence, strong ego, or a 'go get em' personality! For a woman, 'self praise' and 'self promotion' can be looked upon as bragging, showing off, or being 'bossy' or 'bitchy.'

Think about it. If you assess how your day went on any given day, you will undoubtedly come across at least one instance where you you did not advocate for yourself to the best of your abilities (either in the workplace or at home)... OK, maybe more than one instance. But who's counting?

Once we have gone through the assessing stage and acknowledging where we can improve, we start to form your strategy and take time to evaluate body language, written and oral expression—all fundamental and crucial components in knowing how to sell yourself and others. Body language will be covered in a separate chapter, and I guarantee you will rethink the way you move and communicate using your body.

Speaking of Coaching—A Lesson from History

I want to share with you some women who empowered women in history, and remain role models today. If you remember just one fact, share it with friends, colleagues, and family. They will be impressed!

1. In 1820, Susan Brownell Anthony, the first woman to have her picture on an American coin (the silver dollar), formed the National Woman Suffrage Association to fight for women's rights.She was one of the important advocates to be acknowledged by the American government.

2. Let's give thanks to Barbara Walters, who in 1931 became the first female TV anchor on ABC nightly news. She went on to have an extremely successful career and helped bring women into media.

3. A huge inspiration to women everywhere was Amelia Earhart, the first woman to receive the US distinguished flying cross, awarded for becoming the first aviatrix to fly solo across the Atlantic Ocean. She set a huge number of other records and was an early supporter of the equal rights amendment.

4. In the 1800s, Annie Oakley was the most famous female sharpshooter! She was the first American female superstar, having been given the lead role in Buffalo Bill's Wild West show, and she had paid off her mother's mortgage on the family farm by the age of fifteen. Quite the impressive achievement for her era and her age!

5. As of 2016, Shonda Rhimes is arguably the most powerful woman making TV shows. She is the mastermind behind *Grey's Anatomy, Private Practice, Scandal,* and *How To Get Away With Murder.* When receiving the Sherri Lansing Leadership Award at The 2014 Hollywood Reporter's Women in Entertainment Breakfast, she summed up the role of all the women who came before us very nicely:

> From then to now, we've all made such an incredible leap. All of the women, white or black or brown who woke up like this, who came before me in this town. Think of them. Heads up, eyes on the target. Running. Full speed. Gravity be damned. [...] Running, full speed and crashing. Crashing into that ceiling and falling back. Crashing into it and falling back. Into it and falling back. Woman after woman. Each one running and each one crashing. And everyone falling.

How many women had to hit that glass before the first crack appeared? How many cuts did they get, how many bruises? How hard did they have to hit the ceiling? How many women had to hit that glass to ripple it, to send out a thousand hairline fractures? How many women had to hit that glass before the pressure of their effort caused it to evolve from a thick pane of glass into just a thin sheet of splintered ice? So that when it was my turn to run, it didn't even look like a ceiling anymore. I mean, the wind was already whistling through—I could always feel it on my face. And there were all these holes giving me a perfect view to other side. I didn't even notice the gravity, I think it had worn itself away.

So I didn't have to fight as hard. I had time to study the cracks. I had time to decide where the air felt the rarest, where the wind was the coolest, where the view was the most soaring. I picked my spot in the glass and called it my target. And I ran. And when I hit, finally, that ceiling, it just exploded into dust. Like *that*. My sisters who went before me had already handled it. No cuts. No bruises. No bleeding. Making it through the glass ceiling to the other side was simply a matter of running on a path created by every other woman's footprints. I just hit at exactly the right time in exactly the right spot.

Inspired yet? Where are the cracks in your ceiling? Go get 'em girl!

Now what?

If you have gone through the process of answering the questions in Chapter Four, your personal circumstance and an idea of the direction you want your career to head should be a little clearer. If not, don't stress. Head back to the chapter, refresh your memory, and take your time.

When women come to me for for help, they are typically in one of three situations:

1. They're about to negotiate a salary. This might be a starting salary of a new position or they're renegotiating the existing salary as part of a promotion or in general against another company.

2. They might be trying to move up within their company and need to figure out how to do it because they feel stuck.

3. They are looking for a change and are re-evaluating what they are currently doing. This situation is very different from negotiating a new salary or wanting to progress within their current company.

Which scenario are you currently in? Keep this in mind and read on.

Grab your pen and paper, brew a fresh cup of coffee, and get ready to work through the following questions.

You may want to re-evaluate your answers from Chapter Four and treat Chapters Four and Five as the basis of forming your strategy. Now is also a great time to flick back through previous chapters and remind yourself of the journey so far.

1. Accurately assess your current circumstances.

- Do you fit into one of the three scenarios above?
- Do you recognize yourself in one of the examples in Chapter Three?
- Can you identify how you are perceived within your working environment?
- What do you want to achieve and what do you need in order to achieve it? (in monetary terms? Experience?)

2. Do your research and establish what you are worth.

- Refer back to Chapter Five and make sure the concepts are fresh in your mind.
- Focus on research and take time to carry out your own.
- Spend ten minutes a day calling companies within your niche and ask questions. Talk to hiring managers before you even apply. Build pre-emptive rapport.

3. Assess your environment.

- What does the company's financial situation look like?
- When would be the ideal time to bring up a conversation?
- Do you have rapport with your manager?
- Do you have leverage?
- What are your alternatives?
- These questions may take longer than you think to answer, so take your time. After all, this is your career and your worth. This is what you are fighting for, so it's pretty important to know where you want to go.

Statistics Time

Women underestimate their skills and overestimate the risks.

We are all faced with our own voices of self-doubt and criticism, but we will also face it from the outside world. Social media, TV, the workplace, and even the school gates can and will impress their voices of doubt or judgement upon us.

Here are the two statistics that kept repeating themselves when it came to self-doubt:

- The average woman will self-criticize herself at least 8-10 times a day.
- In a single day, 97% of women will be cruel about her body, clothes, or hair.

As women, we are aware of the voices of disruption; so I am not going to dwell on more figures to aid our already overloaded thoughts. Be strong, believe, and read on. Only you can be responsible for your thoughts.

Chapter 8

SPEAK UP WITHOUT SAYING A WORD

Your body communicates as well as your mouth. Don't contradict yourself. —Allen Ruddock

What does body language have to do with knowing and getting your worth? Well, good question!

I am going to let you in on a little secret... body language is incredibly underutilized in interview and negotiation situations, especially by women. I am going to share with you a few subtle and body language signs you can use as part of your strategy. Be aware there is homework in this chapter—I can't do all the work!

Listen to your body

We don't realize that our bodies are always talking and giving away our internal experiences, thoughts, and feelings. Similar to speaking, our body is constantly projecting information whether it be through facial expressions, body movement, how we adjust our hair, or how we dress and carry ourselves.

The difference between spoken language and body language is that the vast majority of the population can't control body language as well as spoken language, and therefore our body can give away our true feelings, intentions, and thoughts, even when we don't want it to. **This nonverbal communication is always happening, but most people don't realize we can use it in order to understand others and to influence the perception others have of us.**

Getting too scientific is beyond the scope of this book, but just know that the limbic system[1] in our brain triggers physical reactions to our emotions that are instantaneous and hard to control. These outward signals give away an accurate representation of our emotions to the external world.

From head to toe, there is always something to decode. Proficiency in knowing how to interpret this language can really give you insight into the emotional state of others and what they're thinking.

You can benefit from guiding your own body language to influence perception. Without even knowing it, you will also have the ability to read other people's body language. For instance, you will often know when someone is feeling stressed by a simple gesture: maybe they run their hands vigorously through their hair or purse their lips together. Look around you and be aware of how people are moving; it's interesting and easy.

Use your body language to your advantage

In the world of interviewing, you can use body language to analyze whether or not you've built rapport with the interviewer. Do they lean into you when you are talking? Are their arms open

---

1. Limbic System: a complex system of nerves and networks in the brain, involving several areas near the edge of the cortex concerned with instinct and mood. It controls the basic emotions (fear, pleasure, anger) and drives (hunger, sex, dominance, care of offspring). Source Wikipedia

and relaxed? These can all be subtle signs your interview is going well.

This is just a brief overview of how to interpret your own body language and that of your interviewer. If you want to learn more, I strongly encourage you to read *What Every Body is Saying* by former FBI Agent Joe Navarro.

You should take these tips and start practicing with them in your daily life, so that, on the day you need to read the subtle signs, you can assess the situation without having to focus too much attention on reading people. Focus on the interview and let your subconscious read the interviewer, making all the assessments for you. In the art of reading body language, practice makes perfect!

Awareness of the Norm

Establish situational awareness and what we call a "normal" baseline. During interview scenarios, you will be able to gauge what someone's baseline behavior is by looking at various ways they act. For example: their breathing patterns.

- Does it change frequently?
- Does their voice or speed of conversation change if they get exasperated or excited?
- Do they talk using their hands in normal conversation?
- Do they have a habit of touching their hair in general conversation?

Essentially, when you establish what their normal behavior is, this will then enable you to analyze their body language through deviations from that normal behavior.

The feet don't lie

Your feet, believe it or not, are a part of your body that assess the situation and react completely from inner feelings and true thoughts. If you are in a group of people sitting together and you really don't want to be in the conversation, your feet will give you away. You may be present and polite, but your feet will be pointing in the opposite direction, ready to escape!

Equally, if you like someone or feel comfortable in your surroundings, your feet will stay put and point to exactly who you want to be talking to. The same goes for someone you are attracted to!

Mind your knees. If you've ever been ready to leave the boardroom or a meeting, you have probably clasped your knees together and placed your palms down on them, as if to say, "That's it, I'm done."

Make some room. Notice how much room people take up with their legs. This is often a trait used by men when they need to give off increased status. Sitting with your legs wide apart makes you feel bigger, stronger, and is a show that you want to be taken seriously or be seen.

Cross over. For most of us, crossing our legs is as natural as brushing our hair in the morning, and it's a sure way of showing we are comfortable in the situation. Take note at which way you are crossing your legs in your next conversation. Crossing them towards the other person usually means you find them interesting or you are attracted to them, and crossing away from the speaker can mean you want to leave or you have lost interest.

Your own personal army—your arms!

I could probably give you an entire chapter on the arms alone. Your arms are one of the biggest giveaways to how you and others are feeling about a situation. They are your protector, they are there to remind you how you are feeling and warn others of your true feelings too. Your arms are your own personal army—willing to stand up for you OR give you away. For instance, if someone throws something at you, your arms are the first thing to react and try to protect you—it's human instinct at its best.

The arm cross: a dead giveaway you are uncomfortable in your situation. This gesture is believed to have a detrimental effect in business and especially in a situation like an interview or meeting. Have you ever been in a meeting that just went on and on, and the next thing you know, you have switched off, sat back in your chair and crossed your arms? It's your brain's way of telling you (and everyone else) that you are done, bored, and ready to leave.

A manager with practice, however, may refuse to cross their arms and purposely refrain from doing so. This is often to show they are not weak or nervous and they want to remain superior with the team or meeting.

Numerous studies have been carried out; it has been proven that people who sit in a meeting or lecture with their arms crossed will learn and retain 40% less than their open-armed counterparts. Plus, as long as someone holds an arms-folded position, a negative attitude will persist.

Homework: Try it out. In your next meeting or social gathering, sit down with crossed arms, even if it's just for twenty minutes, and see how you feel at the end of it. Also take note as to how other people treat you.

> If you want to find the truth, do not listen to the words coming to you. Rather see the body language of the speaker. It speaks the facts not audible. —Bharesh Chhatbar

The hands-in-front-of-zipper fold: very often used by men when they are feeling vulnerable, notoriously used by men in power and usually before they present a speech. The hands rest neatly folded on their zipper almost as a way of saying, "I may humiliate myself when I speak but my crown jewels remain well-protected."

Homework: Set a day aside to see how many people you notice using this hand gesture. It's great practice on reading body language.

The coffee cup of insecurity: Try to take over the world, but first, coffee! One of the most subtle and common ways we protect ourselves is to use our coffee cup. This can be a great tool to find out how comfortable someone is feeling in a meeting or interview. Many business leaders will offer a refreshment in a negotiation scenario; knowing that how their customer or supplier reacts to holding their cup will often give away how they feel the negotiation is going.

For example, if the person is happy and open to how the negotiation is going, they will hold the coffee cup to the side of their body. If they are not comfortable, they will usually hold the coffee cup and move the arm in front of the torso to the opposite side. This is a simple and sneaky but very effective technique used in business.

Homework: In your next negotiation or discussion (this can be at home or within the workplace), give the coffee cup test a go and see what reaction you get.

To touch or not to touch: Some of us are not entirely comfortable with touching. In Europe, it's an expression of greeting, happiness, and acceptance, and touching is widely used as a form of communication. The power of touch is often overlooked and, when used in a subtle and professional way, can be highly effective, whether it's a simple rest on their shoulder, elbow, or a double-handed handshake.

Homework: Next time you are introduced to someone, shake their hand and lightly touch their elbow at the same time, and see what reaction you get and how the rest of the conversation pans out!

The most important part in communication is to hear what isn't being said. —Peter Drucker

Tune into your torso

Our torso is the largest part of our body and, even though our hands and feet steal the limelight, the torso has its part to play. Torso signs, although subtle, are easier to read, as there is only so much it can do.

- Facing you: Conveys interest in you and the conversation
- Slightly tilting away: The person is losing interest
- Turning away completely: You are dismissed and the person wants to move on
- Leaning towards you: A perfect sign the person is interested and engaged in what you are saying
- Leaning away from you: Usually a sign the person wants to move away from you but has not committed to doing so 100%

Homework: Put your torso to the test. Try out a couple of the moves above in a few conversations and see how it makes you feel.

Heads up! In a similar vein, your head can express your true feelings in a situation. For example, have you ever noticed that, when you are sad, you naturally lower your head? Or when you are paying respect to someone or something? In a workplace scenario, lowering the head can express a sign of submission. If the head is lowered but the eyes maintain contact, it can mean the person is sending you a sign of caution or defiance.

Princess Diana used the head lowering and eye gazing expression to her advantage with the ever present and persistent media. She was saying, I am being submissive, but I still have my eyes on you—be wary! Its an expression she is now well-remembered for.

A simple head raise can mean "I am bored," or "What do you mean?" If you can read it at the same time as the facial expression, you usually get a good indication of what someone is saying. In the workplace, you will often find people point their heads at the person of power or the person that is most respected in the room. We naturally point towards people or things we are interested in.

Touching the chin or stroking the nose can often mean someone is in deep thought and seriously considering what you are saying. If you see this during your negotiation, way to go!

Last but by no means least—Face the truth

There are so many expressions that I could spend the next three chapters explaining them all, but let's concentrate on the expressions best-known for reading people and expressing confidence in a professional situation.

- Convey Interest—Hold a steady gaze, along with slightly raised eyebrows and lips lightly pressed together.

- Appear Calm—Relax your facial muscles and hold a steady gaze, perhaps hold a gentle smile.

- Be trustworthy—Hold a slight smile with eyebrows slightly raised.

Do you notice how the above facial expressions are pretty similar? Being in an interview can be daunting, but if you can come across as interested, calm, and trustworthy all from a few facial expressions, you'll be on your way!

Where to go from here

This chapter is a lot to take in (and you should refer back to it when you need to). Do give your homework a shot, as it's great practice for reading body language; you may even find you have a knack for it! Our bodies are primarily there to help and protect us. If you can learn to read yourself and other people, you will be ten steps ahead of most.

Statistics Time

Throughout all aspects of our everyday lives, we communicate using:

- 55% body language
- 38% tone of voice
- 7% words
- You need to maintain eye contact for 60% of the time in order to look interested, but not aggressive.
- In conversation, the speaker maintains eye contact for 40% of the time, whereas the listener maintains eye contact for 75% of the time.
- When a man holds another man's gaze, he is deemed powerful. When a woman holds and man's gaze, she is usually perceived as a flirt.

Need some visuals? No problem—here are some illustrations

by my friend Stephanie Halligan from Art to Self. See if you can figure out the positive from the not-so-positive images.

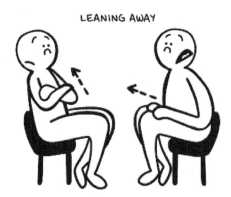

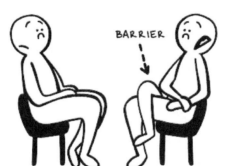

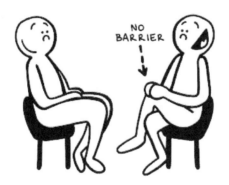

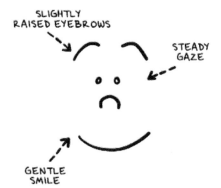

Chapter 9

NEGOTIATION SUMMED UP!

Successful negotiation feels like baking your cake and eating it too. Follow the recipe and you'll be quite satisfied with the outcome. —Olivia Jaras

When it comes down to it, negotiation is being able to read the other person, figure out what they want, and use that information to get what you both want. But if you dig a little deeper, it's about learning to manipulate the situation so that you end up getting what you want without coming across as aggressive. Successful negotiators have the ability to make you feel good about yourself and the negotiation. But what's more, they leave you looking forward to the next negotiation.

If you have followed the chapters and completed the homework throughout the book, you should be in a great place to start to negotiate your worth. We have followed the below basic pattern:

1. Know what you want.

2. Understand what they want.

3. Be aware of the situation around you.

4. Communication is important—verbal and nonverbal.

Meet Amy—Assertive vs. Aggressive

Situations don't always have fairy-tale endings. You sometimes end up kissing a frog and getting nothing but a frog in return. Amy came to me after listening to me speak at an open lecture at one of the top business schools in the world. She was looking to establish her worth within her market sector. We carried out our research and analyzed current market data. I gave her the information and, without giving herself the time to form any strategy, she barged into her boss's office and demanded a raise.

She got a "pity raise" of $200/month. Nice, but not great. If Amy had formed her strategy and assessed her situation following the steps outlined thus far, she could have easily obtained $700/month. Not only did she irritate her boss, but she came across as aggressive and has put to bed any chance of being able to negotiate her worth again within the company any time soon.

Meet Karen—Self-doubt vs. Self-confidence

Karen is a dyslexic MIT molecular engineer who has been involved with some pretty intense government-funded technology. Let's just say even Tom Cruise in *Mission Impossible* would have been impressed!

Because of her dyslexia, she never thought she could amount to much in terms of career. Self-doubt was in her thoughts, actions, and overall persona, and this affected how she was perceived by others and she knew it.

As a young woman, Karen persevered with her studies and career and made it through MIT and beyond. She was smart, successful, and an incredible asset to any company. After a short time, she found herself at the negotiating table with top-secret government agencies. Yep, she was that good! It was at this table, when the officials offered "him" a salary and role in the management team, that she realized that they didn't really think this "woman" was part of the invention. They thought Karen was merely representing the scientist on the project... when she was the scientist all along!

Even though Karen tried to explain, and the top-secret agents were embarrassed by their mistake, the deal they offered Karen was nowhere near in line with what they had offered "him." So Karen walked away from the negotiating table highly demoralized, because she didn't counter their offer.

This was a tricky case, because we had to work on going back to the negotiating table after everyone else thought the negotiation was done. We worked on what Karen really wanted out of the negotiation, but we also had to focus on how she carried herself, what she wore, and worked on re-branding her persona. Even though I am a huge advocate that we should stay true to ourselves, sometimes you need to manipulate how others perceive you in order to get what you want. As I've said before: **If you don't believe your story, why should anyone else?**

Meet Melissa—Verbal vs. Non Verbal

We all know nonverbal behavior plays a big part in how you are perceived. When it comes to negotiation, coming across as confident, calm, and assured will give you a good start.

Melissa was keen to negotiate a raise during her upcoming annual review, and once we had carried out the research and figured out her worth, we worked on her strategy to approach her boss. She knew her colleagues were being paid more than her, she just didn't have the courage to approach her peers.

For Melissa, it was all about the body language. As a child, she had been living up to perfectionist parents, constantly reminded she could do better, and this bled into her adult life too. Enough was never good enough. Her posture was low-slung, she struggled to look people in the eye, and she fidgeted a lot when she was nervous. In a negotiation scenario, these simple movements can go against you, it's as fickle as that.

After a few weeks of working together, some confidence boosting, and with the realization she was only asking for what she was truly worth, Melissa realized she could be calm, confident, and self-assured. She just needed to believe it herself first, before trying to convince others. The change was inspiring; it was noticeable without her even saying a word.

What did she do on the day of the negotiation? Melissa had great joy in telling me this story. For her, this boost in self-confidence was just as big a deal as negotiating the actual raise! Melissa entered the room and smiled, made gentle, warm eye contact, and slowly leaned into the situation assertively, but not aggressively. She calmly sat down, and was on queue with all the points she wanted to make to her boss. She was completely in the moment and aware of what she was saying, and her body language: head held high and steady, arms gently rested on the table.

Knowing the environment she wold be negotiating in, we planned for Melissa to gently mimic the person's body language and gestures. If they nodded their head, she would discretely nod too. If they brushed their hair, she would do the same.

If you mimic another person's actions, it increases the instinct for the other person to relate to and like you. Disclaimer: this has to be carried out gently and not in an obvious, weird way!

It also gave Melissa something to focus on apart from her own nerves. Melissa did not fidget, fiddle, or chew on her lip; the mimic distraction worked and she felt calm and relaxed. All of this, coupled with the knowledge and research about her worth, led to Melissa walking away with a $12k per year raise, with the option of reviewing her salary again in twelve months time.

Coaching Tips—Homework time!

This is just a bit of fun (and a great excuse for me to get the word "negotiation" in again). How well can you negotiate? Tick them off as you go!

Next time you are out in a friendly situation, ask for something from a complete stranger. It could be anything.

Expect pushback with these exercises. But, being the savvy negotiator that you are, use your background research and your verbal and nonverbal cues to get things done your way.

Get in contact with your credit card company and ask if they can give you a better interest deal, since you could always go to one of their competitors. How much leverage do you have?

Offer to make or get a coffee for a colleague you have never spoken to before.

Take a friend out for lunch where you usually pick up the bill and ask if they can pay half this time.

If you are hosting friends or family for dinner, ask to make it a potluck and suggest people bring items instead of you cooking everything.

Ask your neighbor if you can borrow or have something—maybe some milk, sugar, or something you need for the garden.

Take five minutes each day thinking about a situation that did not go your way. What could you have done better or how could you have reacted better? Think about verbal and nonverbal communication.

Introspect a little bit. Actively try to change some external behavior that you know has a not-so-positive impact on the way you come across.

Open yourself to a bit of criticism and ask for someone's opinion on how they perceive your body language came across in a situation. It could be at home or in the workplace.

Negotiate something with a family member. Maybe you want your partner to take the kids to their soccer practice this weekend while you get a massage. How would you use body language to communicate; what does your partner get out of it?

Statistics Time

People assume negotiating is often tackled in a dominant and aggressive way to get what you want from a situation, however I think we have just proven, in successful negotiations, this is not the case.

Yet, so many women are still shying away from negotiations. Why?!

You've heard this before, but this time, in numbers. Women are often forced to toe the line between masculine and feminine roles when it comes to their salary. If we don't ask, we are often perceived as being "girly" and "weak," and if we do ask, we are deemed as "aggressive" or "unlike-able." Doomed if you don't, damned if you do.

- Over 60% of females in the workplace do not know how to negotiate.
- 18% of women feel they will come across as pushy.
- 8% of women worry about losing their jobs.
- 31% of women said they were "uncomfortable" with negotiating their salaries.

These figures all pretty much tell the same story. We are afraid to negotiate. Be the change you want to see!

Chapter 10

CRAFT YOUR STRATEGY

Strategy is a fancy word for coming up with a long term
plan and putting it into action. —Ellie Pidot

By now, the wheels in your brain are probably turning, and you
are anxious to get going and start negotiating your raise,
negotiating different hours, or applying for that new job and
getting what you're worth. This is where we provide you with a
road map so that you can plot your own unique strategy.

"Every battle is won before it is fought." —Sun Tzu

My advice is that you take at least thirty days to carry out research and go through the strategy development in this book. If you are new to advocating for yourself or simply have enough time to work through the book, I strongly suggest you take as much time as you need to make sure every step is taken care of and cemented properly before you go on to the next step. Your salary depends on it!

Plan your journey to success

At this point, you will just need to remind yourself of what it is you want to achieve from your own unique situation. Planning will make the difference between success and failure. Use what you have learned in the previous chapters, read through your answers, and feel empowered by the statistics.

Feel ready, get motivated, and create your own road map to success.

Days 1 – 10—Get polished

- Polish up your résumé with the guidance I have given you in this book, remember to make sure that your strengths shine!
- Once you have done a thorough job with this, look at the position description in question. In an unbiased way, judge yourself relative to the role.
- Review your cover letter, are you repeating what you have already said in your résumé?

Days 3 – 10—Figure out your worth

- Research time. Use the guidance in this book to figure out what you are worth.
- In the United States, there's always the US Census Bureau data as well as a myriad of other online salary search engines.
- Reach out to at least two individuals (hopefully one male) that you might know in the industry doing your same job. They can be colleagues at the same company as you, but

only if you think this would not jeopardize your ability to negotiate.

- Email two other companies to ask them for their feedback, using the email/call guide we provided you in Chapter 5.

If you would rather have someone do all of this for you, let the pros with paid survey data do the work instead at www.salarycoaching.com. We'll help with your strategy as well! Let our experts price you relative to your relevant market.

Days 1 – 30—Become an awareness ninja

- Start becoming aware of the way that you communicate with your body.
- What does the way you dress say about you?
- What does the way you speak or move say about how people perceive you?
- What strengths do you have in terms of using body language to build rapport?
- What aspect of your nonverbal communication should you consider addressing in order for you to be the most persuasive non-verbal communicator out there?

Take a few days to think about it, try to master your own actions and be aware of them, and observe how people react to your body language.

If you are preparing for a negotiation in your current workplace, start observing those individuals with whom you will be negotiating. Watch your boss and your boss's boss.

- Do they tend to be dominant in conversations?

- What gets their attention? What topics get them in a good mood?
- How could you best utilize your strengths to come across as persuasive and build rapport with them?

Be sneaky and deliberate. Observe. Don't let anyone know that you're working on this in the office. Always try to be fully aware of how they operate and read them through their body language. Hands, feet, torso, and eyes—what do they say?

If you are preparing for an interview and you have never met the individuals before, research the company, understand the culture, and gauge what it is that they look for in candidates through all the information you can get.

- Is it a very dull organization? Uptight? Spunky?
- Is it very lax about regulations?
- What is the culture like?

Get a better idea of how you could best portray yourself within the interview.

Doing It "Like a Girl"—Crafting Your Strategy

Visualization is a great tool! Use the tools we have provided you throughout this book, visualize the different case scenarios and outcomes based on how well you utilize and test the tactics we've covered.

Think of the best case scenario, the worst case, and the midpoint. It may be that none of these scenarios you conceive pan out, but at least you'll have a backup plan, and you won't be caught off guard. For example: Despite your resilience to pushback, you are just getting nowhere with your boss. But you know this is a company you really love and want to stick with. Establish that your goal is to continue with them in a capacity that is effective and fair to both of you, and "Let's revisit this conversation in a month or so?" Regroup and revise your strategy based on this experience and come in twice as ready and powerful as you were the first time. You know your worth, make them realize it too! Visualizing and mentally preparing yourself will allow you to keep your cool and stay comfortable throughout the process.

Take time to think what your body language looks like in each case; will it change based on how well the scenario is going?

- Think about how you build rapport without antagonizing the interviewer and getting them to like you.
- In order to build the positive rapport, what should your words sound like?
- What does the worst case scenario look like?
- How can you most effectively turn this negative into simply a postponed yes?
- Can you take the job now and set the stage for a salary review in the near future?
- Can you generate buy-in and work together with your manager to get what you deserve?

Play all the scenarios in your head, and voice your role out loud. Play the scenarios WITH your body language. Use a family member or friend and practice what you will say and how you plan on reacting. Role play is a really effective way of getting over nerves, and hearing the sound of your own voice can make you feel more confident.

Dress to Impress

Fashion is not something that exists in dresses
only. Fashion is in the sky, in the street, fashion has to
do with ideas, the way we live, what is happening.
—Coco Chanel

We haven't really covered clothing thus far. I wanted to save it for this chapter as, ultimately, it should be the final part of your preparation.

Clothes are an expression of our personality. Many use clothing to hide or show off their bodies and, for women, clothes can cause great anxiety or great excitement! We are all judged on our appearance, whether that's fair or not. However, we can manipulate what we wear to help our situation.

A company culture will have a big impact on how you will dress in your workplace. For example, you may work in a company that encourages casual dress, so walking around in a power suit will make you stand out from the crowd in the wrong way. Formal suits are not always the way to go—research has shown that people who wear a slightly different or brighter color outfit are perceived as more attractive and confident. This could be a huge bonus if you are looking to work in a creative industry.

Model your own style. Look for role models within your sector and see how they dress. Realize how you feel when you put on a smart, well-fitted jacket or a cute dress. Our clothes can put our minds in the right place. Studies have shown people in more formal attire get served more quickly in shops and are usually judged as more intelligent and academic. Women who dressed in a smart and slightly masculine style were perceived as more forceful and aggressive and were more likely to get hired.

As you prepare for negotiation or interview day, be mindful

of the effect your clothes can have. Your choice will change your mindset and the perception you give others.

Essentially, research, practice, pick out an outfit that conveys the right message, and go get 'em!

A note on LGBTQIA women negotiations. This is a topic that my team and I are currently working on and I feel compelled to include a word about it here, because we are all part of the same community. At Salary Coaching, we have carried out some client-based research on salary negotiations for LGBTQIA women and have found that there often seems to be positive discrimination within this group. Particularly, we have found:

- Your negotiation outcome odds increase if your interviewer makes the assumption that you are out of maternity risk.
- If the interviewer identifies you with a more masculine role from the onset of negotiations, they will be more receptive to assertiveness throughout the process.

As you can tell, the data on LGBTQIA women and salary negotiations is limited. If you, or women you know have data or narratives to share, please reach out to us at www.salarycoaching.com, we'd love to hear from you!

Is today the day?

"Success is often achieved by those who don't know failure is inevitable." —Coco Chanel

"This is your world. Shape it or someone else will." —Gary Lew

This book has opened up the key secrets to negotiating your

salary. But the only way you will change your life and your salary in the long run is when you decide to take action to raise your own standards. You may have breezed through this book, and are now getting ready to use it as a coffee table decoration rather than take irretractable action to improve your career life... And that's alright—not everyone is ready to raise their own standard yet. But when you've had enough, when you find yourself at rock-bottom, you know you will be ready.

When you are no longer willing to tolerate selling yourself short, when you are no longer willing to be used by others, and you are ready to earn what you deserve, you will decide to take action.

When you realize, just as the women who cracked the glass ceiling before us, that you decide what legacy you will leave for women and girls for generations to come, you'll finally decide to stop selling yourself short. Remember that we need you on the other side of current statistics.

Close your own wage gap so that you can help other women *close the gender pay gap.*

———————

Let's continue the conversation!

Email me your thoughts: olivia@salarycoaching.com.

Acknowledgements

I'd like to acknowledge my husband Paul for his never-ending patience and ability to put up with me pulling in 10,000 directions all at once. I'd also like to acknowledge my girls—you are my eternal source of inspiration.

Katie Barnes—For your research, collaboration, and help finding the words to express myself.

Alberto Rodriguez—For your expertise and generosity as a photographer.

Hannah Joslin—For helping me navigate the world of editing and publishing.

Ana Mata-Murray—For your endless willingness to help and expand our cause.

The Salary Coaching Team—For keeping our mission alive and well!

And a special acknowledgement to life and all the good and bad that it has brought me. Without all those trials and tribulations, I would have never come this far.

About the Author

Olivia lives in Hanover, New Hampshire, and is the mother of two young girls. Though she was born in the US, Olivia grew up in Santiago, Chile, and quickly became keenly aware at a young age of the impact of social imbalances. She obtained her undergraduate degree in International Relations from Tufts University; and later earned her Master's from George Washington University in Latin American Business Development, as well as her MBA from Bellarmine College. She is also a Certified Compensation Professional (CCP), the widely accepted designation for experts in the field of salaries and compensation.

Olivia founded Salary Coaching LLC after spending the better part of a decade setting salaries. From working at one of the world's largest HR consulting firms, to Latin America's largest development bank, to later holding a senior role in the compensation department at an Ivy League institution, Olivia has an insider perspective on how salaries are set and how employees are compensated.

Over the years working in compensation, Olivia began noticing that even though she was being completely unbiased when recommending salary ranges to hiring managers for their identified hires, when a woman was hired, she inevitably came in towards the lower end of the range, while men were generally higher. In talking with the hiring managers, the answer was always along the lines of "She never really asked for more," or, "She seemed so excited to just get the job that she didn't even ask about it...."

Realizing that this was the key to closing the gender wage gap, Olivia founded Salary Coaching for Women, making it her career to teach women to advocate for themselves in the workplace as well as providing a peek into the insider secrets of compensation. Olivia and her Salary Coaching Team have been very successful in helping women earn more money, get promoted, find the job of their dreams, and advocate for themselves at work all over the world.

Olivia enjoys racing triathlons. This is a hobby she picked up with her brother during college. Yet after gaining 60 pounds during each of her pregnancies, and the untimely and sudden death of her brother, she decided she could either settle in her sadness or pick herself back up and chase her dreams. Living proof that dreams can be achieved, Olivia is now a TEAM USA athlete and is representing the country at the World Triathlon Championships in 2017.

Made in the USA
Monee, IL
13 March 2022

92812514R00069